How to Build a Friendly Robot

A Machine Explains What It Means to be Human

A Philosophical Novel

Bob Kohn

Theoria Books
New York

The names of real people, businesses, characters, and places, including trademarks and service marks, are used in this book and on its cover. They are either the products of the author's imagination or are used fictitiously, descriptively, and critically to further the story or to explore the newsworthy and philosophical ideas discussed in this book. The Google name and logo are a registered trademarks of Google, Inc. and the IBM name and logo are registered trademarks of IBM, Inc. Neither the book nor its contents are authorized, approved, sponsored by, or is otherwise associated with, Google, Inc. or IBM, Inc. or any of their affiliated companies. *Theoria*® is a registered trademark of Theoria Publishing Co. Cover art includes a silhouette image by Michel Sanca licensed from Shutterstock.com and modified by Theoria Books.

Published in the United States by Theoria Books, a division of Theoria Publishing Co., New York, NY

Library of Congress Cataloging-in-Publication Data

Kohn, Bob
How to Build a Friendly Robot: A Machine Explains What It Means to Be Human
/ Bob Kohn

ISBN 978-0-9721545-1-2 (trade paperback)
ISBN 978-0-9721545-2-9 (ebook)

To Mortimer J. Adler
whose wisdom and understanding
inspired this story

1

Scene of the Crime

Monday, June 21, 2032

Google-IBM Android Kills Inmate at Manhattan Psychiatric Ward

NEW YORK—A human-like android named "Robbie," engineered and released last week by Google-IBM, killed a patient last evening at the Manhattan Psychiatric Center on Wards Island in New York City. The patient, 34-year old Charles F. Collins, suffered a broken neck as the android attempted to restrain him with a choke hold. A spokesperson for the company insisted the death was not the result of any malfunction on the part of the droid. "It was merely an accident that occurred while Robbie was defending human life under extreme circumstances," he said. "Any human could have made the same mistake."

The incident occurred during a brawl involving several patients in Ward-3 of the psychiatric center. Patients held in Ward-3 were either incompetent to stand trial or proven not guilty by reason of insanity. "Rapists, killers, cannibals, the worst of the worst," one of the center's orderlies told the Times under condition of anonymity. "Incurably insane. Don't know right from wrong. Psychotics and sociopaths, dangerously clever people who have no place in civilized society." The center is surrounded by a 20-foot high chain link fence topped by loops of razor wire and observation towers equipped with spotlights and surveillance cameras.

Charles Collins was committed for murdering his husband, who he suspected of cheating on him. He fed his husband's remains to his in-laws who thought their son was in Asia on business. Two years ago, he attempted to kill one of the staff psychiatrists at Ward-3. Collins stabbed the doctor with a fork and bit off half his ear.

Because of the danger to the staff of Ward-3, the City of New York leased two androids from Google-IBM—Robbie and an android named "Adam"—to serve as orderlies at the facility.

Last evening, Collins picked a fight with another inmate, which kicked off a violent brawl. The entire scene was captured by surveillance video. In the midst of the melee, a doctor asked the robot Adam to restrain Collins, but Collins took out the droid with a swift uppercut to the chin. The blow dislodged the droid's head and the machine slumped to the floor inoperable. When asked to bring Collins under control, Robbie successfully dodged Collins's violent swings, spun the patient around, and secured him with a police-style choke hold. But the force of the hold, according to one of the orderly's present, snapped the patient's neck and Collins died moments later.

Just two weeks ago, Google-IBM released their new generation of droids under a pilot program approved by the cities of New York, San Francisco, and Miami. Each city permitted the company to deploy 32 human-like machines to perform various jobs, public and private, from simple to complex. Some served in restaurants; others assisted the elderly in retirement homes. As a condition to obtaining their permit to operate the new androids on the streets of New York City, Google-IBM agreed to deploy two of the machines on a gratis basis for use at the Manhattan Psychiatric Center.

As required by the federal Robotics Act of 2025, each droid is monitored continuously by a human "minder" located at a Google-IBM robotics facility, providing constant human oversight, 24/7. A minder must be on hand in the event human intervention was required. If a humanoid were faced with a decision that might affect the safety of any person or property, the droid's minder has options: he could issue a counter-command, take manual control of the android, disable it, or, of course, just watch.

Behind each android's human-like façade is a vast artificial intelligence operating system called Watson-5. The company calls it the "real brain" of these machines. It is through Watson-5 that each droid receives a periodic update to its OS. The droids also continually tap into Watson-5's vast database of object identifiers, transaction data, maps, videos, and other information it may need to obey human commands and complete assigned tasks. And whenever a droid is required to perform some processing-intensive function—such as playing chess, catching a football, or having a conversation—it can tap into Watson-5's distributed server grid for additional information or processing power. Google-IBM touts the system as the most advanced artificial intelligence program in the world.

Since last night's incident, all 32 of the androids deployed in New York City have been recalled to the Google-IBM's robotics facility in Chelsea pending investigation by authorities. Recalls in San Francisco and Miami have not been confirmed. Federal regulatory authorities could not be reached for comment.

2

The Company Lawyer

Shortly after 7AM the next morning, Audrey Paris, senior corporate counsel for Google-IBM's Robotics development team, was sitting in her cubicle on the fifth floor of the firm's Chelsea facility in Manhattan, her mind sped by coffee and dark brown eyes focused on her viewscreen. She had just watched the surveillance videos one more time and was now looking at a live view of the android holding room in the basement of the building.

There stood 31 motionless androids, each wearing a white Kevlar jump suit, zipped up in front to an open collar, with a blue stripe running down the sides of the arms and legs. The Google-IBM logo was embroidered on their left chest pocket. They were identical, except that above the logo was the droid's nickname embroidered in black. Names like Robbie, C-3PO, and Spock. The droids were each standing in its assigned niche, eyes shut, back to the wall, secured by a magnetic attractor. Adam's niche stood eerily vacant.

Rushing the launch was foolish, Audrey thought. But the engineers insisted upon beta testing the bots in the real world. So now, in a flash, an engineering problem became a legal problem. Her problem.

The upgrade to Watson-5 was considered the most important technological leap since Alan Turing first envisioned digital computing in the 1940's. The difference? Unlike Watson-4, the new version was given access to its own source code: if Watson-5 ran into a tough problem, it could solve it by simply rewriting itself. It was the technology's not-so-secret sauce. It was the key to the machine's passing the Turing Test.

Audrey sat back, arms folded, a smartly attractive woman in her early thirties with long brown hair pulled to the side and knotted up behind her left ear. How was it possible, she thought, that a machine—made of mere circuit boards and software algorithms—could actually pass the Turing Test? She witnessed it with her own eyes: objective judges were deceived by Watson-5, hidden behind a screen, into thinking that they were conversing with a human being. Okay, the results were controversial, but who was she to believe: the skeptics or her own eyes? She sided with the skeptics.

Audrey had been working closely with the Robotics engineers for over three years, but still, with all she had come to know about natural language processing, probability analysis, and sequential decision theory, she didn't buy into the hype. The Turing Test only proved that a machine could fake it. It could never really think like a human.

And that, Audrey thought, is where the engineers were making a huge mistake. She recalled her endless debates with Keith King, the project's lead engineer, about "friendly A.I."

"They're self-taught, the safest tools ever built," Keith insisted. He had short hair, neither white nor grey, but dyed a shiny silver. "The learning algorithm will help them learn human values."

"Human values?" Audrey replied. "What the hell does that mean?"

"What does it matter? They'll just figure out how to behave properly on their own."

Audrey didn't believe that for a second. "How's that supposed to work?"

"Like everything else," Keith replied. "By observation, like a child learns in kindergarten that it's not fair to hog up all the crayons."

That approach, as Audrey tried to explain to Keith *ad nauseam*, was fundamentally flawed: humans don't always do the right thing. Children will fight over crayons; adults will fight over far more trivial matters, like land, money, and power. Whatever the right values are, she said, must be hard-coded into the droid's utility function like instincts in an animal—a fixed set of laws and behavioral rules, which the machine must obey regardless of what you tell it to do. Prod a horse to jump on a man lying on the ground. It won't do it. Even if you beat the animal, it just won't budge.

That was the first hurdle, Audrey thought. Machines must be programmed, like instincts in an animal, to disobey when commanded to do harm.

But what is *harm*? That was the other challenge. She knew it can't just be hurt feelings; otherwise, an intelligent machine would never beat us at chess. Nor can the threshold of harm be mere physical injury; otherwise, the machine could never perform surgery, which requires cutting human flesh. Nothing she studied in law school came close to preparing her for the world in which she found herself. Justice, she was taught, was the greatest of all reflections on human nature: if men and women were angels, we wouldn't need law. But we're not. So, laws are needed to discourage us from harming one another. But what about our machines? How do we make them safe?

Audrey never pretended to have the whole thing figured out, but she was continually frustrated by Keith's utter self-assuredness. To his mind, he was not only right, everyone else was wrong—especially the lawyers. A "necessary evil," he once said, referring to Audrey's role on the team. It was one thing for him to dismiss her legal advice, but when she ventured into machine ethics, she had no standing in his court. None whatsoever. Artificial morality was a problem for mathematicians, he insisted, not lawyers.

But Audrey wasn't buying it, at least not quite yet. Indeed, the engineers had pushed the machine into another realm, a higher realm of intelligence. But had they gone too far? No one really knew, but it would be foolish, Audrey thought, to blindly trust the new technology. At least until we better understood what these machines really were and how they worked. Machines are just tools, she agreed. They are useful and could be made safe, somehow, but it was a huge mistake to anthropomorphize them. They don't think like humans and they never will.

She snapped out of her detached gaze and returned her thoughts to the task at hand. She had to think through her legal strategy. Government regulators were on their way and it was her job to keep the feds off the company's back while the engineers figured out what went wrong.

She pictured Keith pacing, wondering what happened: "Damn test suites. Watson has more bugs than a tropical island." *The moron*, Audrey thought, the problem was more basic than that. It's the design, she warned. Now, Keith had a disaster on his hands. The negative publicity will be a nightmare. The lawsuits worse. Yes, the lawsuits. In a civil lawsuit brought by Collin's heirs, if he has any, the company would be held to a strict liability standard for the defective design of its machine. The product liability suit is coming, for sure.

And then there would be the Manhattan District Attorney looking to charge the company with a crime. He's been looking for an excuse for years. Murder? No way, an impossible case. Where's the intent? The act was done by an autonomous machine making its own decisions. Criminal negligence? Reckless endangerment? Perhaps. The machine is an instrumentality of the company and, to convict the company, the D. A. only needs to prove gross recklessness. The company might be vulnerable on that score, but we'd fight it tooth and nail. Besides, the droids were sent to Ward-3 as a test. The city agreed to assume a reasonable risk given the worthy goal: to replace orderlies who were being kicked, beaten and cut up in the most dangerous job in the state.

An alert crossed her screen as her watch vibrated. A call was coming in from Marsha Shaw, an old colleague of Audrey's when the two worked together in the U.S. Attorneys' office in Manhattan. Marsha was now the chief federal prosecutor for the Southern District of New York and had been trying to lure Audrey back to government service. Audrey missed the thrill of the courtroom, but it wasn't time. She repeatedly declined Marsha's offers. *No*, was Audrey's last answer, at least not until her stock options were vested. That was months ago. Nothing has changed, but apparently, Marsha wasn't giving up.

Audrey tapped her screen, "Hey, Marsha."

"Hey, honey. How's corporate life treating you?"

"Well enough," Audrey replied. "Long hours, but at least the pay is lousy."

"Ha, I bet," laughed Marsha. "Anyway, it's good to hear your voice and I'm glad we'll have a chance to work on something together again."

"Sure," replied Audrey. "But this isn't a good time for me. Could we try for lunch next week?"

"Things are moving faster than that. We need to speak about the case right now."

"The case?" asked Audrey.

"The homicidal robot."

Robot? Marsha must be confused, Audrey thought. *What case?* Audrey held her questions in check. "Yes, right. Brain cramp."

"So," continued Marsha, "I assume you heard from the D.A.'s office that they referred the case to us. It seems we have exclusive jurisdiction."

"I see," said Audrey. Yes, now she got it. Under the Federal Robotics Act, all cases involving highly intelligent machines must be tried in federal, instead of state court. The New York District Attorney, by law, must send the case the U.S. Attorneys' Office. That means Marsha, and Marsha didn't waste any time.

"We've seen the police reports and the video, and the staff has recommended we prosecute."

That was fast, thought Audrey. "What's the rush?"

"Off the record?"

"Of course."

"We're worried about a server wipe."

Marsha may have trusted Audrey, but, apparently, not Google-IBM. The company, always a step ahead of government forensic experts, could make records disappear without a trace. "Don't worry, I won't let that happen," replied Audrey.

"Still."

"What are the charges?" Audrey asked.

"One count of involuntary manslaughter, one count of criminal negligence, and one count of reckless endangerment against the company."

That was to be expected, Audrey thought. But then came the ringer.

"The same against the robot, plus a one count of second degree murder."

Marsha couldn't be serious. "Did you say murder? Against the droid?"

"We understand they're programmed to obey the law," replied Marsha. "Justice thinks we need to establish a real incentive for that."

The DOJ must be deranged, Audrey thought. Trying a machine for murder? The trial would be a total farce. "Incentive? How do you propose to punish a machine?"

"You tell me," replied Marsha. "Restrict their freedom. Unplug 'em. They put down dangerous dogs, don't they?"

"But they don't put the dog on trial," replied Audrey.

"Look, decision made," said Marsha.

Okay, thought Audrey. Inevitable, yes, but not easy for the prosecution. It would be a case of first impression. Marsha had a lot to prove. And the media attention—. Wait! This wasn't the DOJ, this was all Marsha's doing. Audrey was sure of it now. She studied her opponent's giddy smile, neatly cropped blonde hair, and olive-shaped hazel green eyes that seemed to sparkle on her view screen. Marsha Elisabeth Shaw, 42, a prosecutor for the U.S. Attorney's Office in Manhattan for twelve years. Now she led it. Lawyers from that office have gone on to become Justices of the Supreme Court, U.S. Senators, and mayors of New York City. Yes, of course. Marsha had been waiting for the right case to come along to make her mark. This, no doubt, was going to be the one. She had tried lots of securities fraud, tax evasion, and racketeering cases, but never one for murder. And never one like this.

If this thing went to court, it could take on the dimensions of the Scopes monkey trial. Marsha was riding the case of a lifetime. And so, it suddenly occurred to Audrey, was she. But how would she defend it? The whole scene at the psychiatric center was recorded. Had the company been reckless? Of course, it had. The engineers were notorious for launching products too soon. This was no exception. How could she set her own feelings about that aside? How could she defend her clients with all the zeal that's professionally required of her?

She had a lot to reconcile, but it all would have to wait. Her job now was to get as much information out of Marsha as she could. Audrey knew that all Marsha needed was a quick plea bargain. She'll get the worldwide attention she needs at her press conference with photos of the droid appearing in handcuffs. That'll do the trick. Marsha never intended to hold a trial. That much Audrey knew.

"What's it going to take to put this behind us?" Audrey asked.

"Guilty pleas and a $500 million dollar fine." She paused. "Each."

The fine was over ten times what the federal sentencing guidelines called for. "You really think you can get a grand jury to indict a *machine*?"

"It doesn't matter what the grand jury does. We're comfortable that we'll get past the preliminary hearing. Probable cause will be a slam dunk."

Audrey was reading the tea leaves. It seemed Marsha wasn't entirely confident about getting an indictment.

Perhaps the grand jury has already signaled some push back. That's why Marsha's filing a criminal complaint. All she needs is a federal judge to agree there was probable cause to charge the droid. The video should remove any doubt about that.

"The plan is to charge and arrest the robot whether or not the grand jury bites."

"Fair enough," replied Audrey. "When do you want your perp walk?"

"We're filing the complaint later this morning."

"This morning?"

"We should be ready to arrest your robot at 11am. Could you have him ready in the lobby?"

"Can you send me the complaint?"

"The second it's filed."

"Would you delay the filing until we can negotiate a plea?"

"No. The ball's rolling on that. We're filing within the hour."

Audrey thought quickly. She had to buy some time, at least enough for the company to prepare for the PR hit. "Could you pick up the droid at 1pm?"

Marsha paused a moment. Audrey was hoping she wouldn't ask for something in return. Then Marsha delivered: "Sure thing."

Whew. No strings attached. It might be the last favor she'll get from her old partner in anti-crime, but Audrey was grateful. "You'll let me attend the booking?"

"Can't wait to see you," replied Marsha. "It'll be like old times."

"Yeah, just like old times," said Audrey, ending the call.

Audrey let Marsha assume that she'd be leading the company's legal defense. Audrey was now determined to make that assumption a reality. Besides, she needed to be on the right side of this issue. And the right side, strangely enough, was working for the defense. Androids should not be treated like human beings under the law. She would have to explain why and make it stick. All the way up to the Supremes, if necessary.

3

The Charges

Minutes later came the call she was waiting for. Josh Friedman, Google-IBM's Chief Legal Officer, came online, along with Morgan Wang, the company's head of litigation, both in a conference room in Mountain View. Morgan, a patent lawyer, had been recruited five years ago to manage the hundreds of lawsuits the company defended annually. Audrey briefed them on her fortuitous call from Marsha. While she was talking, the criminal complaint came in. They looked it over together, but Audrey was the only one on the call with criminal law chops.

"They charged the damn machine?" Josh was shaking his head in disbelief, understandably. "What the hell's with that?"

"Our PR worked," said Audrey. "They threw our hype right back at us. The droids have human intelligence, so they must have human obligations."

"What difference does it make?" said Morgan. "Let's just pay the fine and get the hell out."

"That's not what Travis wants to do," said Josh. Travis Dixon was the company's CEO. "We can settle the charge against the company, but the droid has to fight."

"What for?" Morgan asked.

"He's thinking long term. If we don't take a tough stance, we'll never hear the end of these suits."

"The company will get sued anyway," said Morgan.

"No one cares if the company gets sued," said Josh. "Putting one of our products on trial is another matter."

"Travis is right," interjected Audrey. "We can never admit this machine is legally human."

"But it's programmed to obey the law," replied Morgan. "I don't see how this makes a difference. We should just cop a plea and get this behind us."

"Decision made," said Josh. "The corporation can settle, but the bot will have his day in court. Let's move on."

Morgan turned to Audrey. "When's the preliminary hearing?"

"Two weeks," she replied. "We'll get a date at today's arraignment."

"That doesn't sound like a lot of time," replied Josh. "We need a plan."

That was the opening Audrey needed. It was her opportunity to seize control of the defense and that only required credibility and leadership. "I'll tell Marsha the corporation will offer a plea of *no contest* and pay a fine. She'll ask for nine figures. I'll offer eight. Our objective is to avoid the word *guilty*."

"Think she'll take under a hundred million?" asked Morgan.

"No, but she'll take half of what she's asking for." Audrey exuded confidence and she wasn't faking it.

"What about the droid?" asked Josh.

"I'll tell Marsha the robot will see her in court." Audrey covered her mouth with the back of her hand and laughed at the thought. In her wildest dreams she could never have imagined such a situation.

"What do you think prosecutor will do?" asked Josh.

"She'll go for the money and settle with the corporation," Audrey replied. "I think she's really after the droid."

"Can we settle before they make the arrest?" asked Morgan.

"If you're thinking we can avoid the perp walk, no way. The feds will be here at one o'clock with an arrest warrant."

"But what about the press?" asked Josh. "We can't keep it quiet."

"Announce immediately," advised Audrey.

"Agreed," said Morgan. "That should take the air out of the media balloon."

"And control the spin," said Audrey. "The droid's our property, a machine. We're telling it what to do. It's not acting on its own."

"What will they do with the droid?" asked Josh. "Put it behind bars?"

"They'll take him downtown and book him like any other criminal," said Audrey. "We'll try to avoid jail—"

"Wait," interrupted Morgan. "Don't they know the bot's fully integrated with Watson?"

"Marsha won't let the facts get in the way of a publicity opportunity," said Audrey. "She'll try to personalize this thing. The feds will cuff him, drive him down to 26 Federal Plaza, take mug shots, fingerprints—"

"Fingerprints?" asked Morgan. "Do the bots even *have* them?"

There was a brief silence. The androids looked just like humans. Indeed, the engineers were meticulous about making them appear indistinguishable from us, making every effort to eliminate the so-called "uncanny valley," that eerie feeling you get when you're looking at humanoid that just misses the mark in its likeness to a real person. But fingerprints? Who looks at fingerprints?

"Not our problem," shrugged Audrey.

"I trust they'll read the droid its legal rights," said Josh.

"Of course," she replied. "The Magistrate Judge will do it again later at the arraignment."

"Can a robot really have rights?" asked Morgan.

"Well," Audrey replied, "if it has legal responsibilities, it must have legal rights. This is why we have to fight it. If machines have rights, then what about the right to liberty? We could lose control of these things."

"Didn't that android on *Star Trek* win his freedom?" asked Morgan.

Star Trek? He was making the same mistake as the engineers, anthropomorphizing these things. "Earth to Morgan. These are machines, not humans."

Josh laughed. Morgan looked at his tablet. "I've just pulled up the Thirteenth Amendment. It's not limited to human beings."

Technically, he was right. The Constitution uses the passive voice: *Neither slavery nor involuntary servitude . . . shall exist within the United States.*

"But the intent," said Josh. "It has to be limited to human beings, right?"

"Of course," replied Audrey, though she only feigned certainty. She had heard about those cases brought by animal rights activists claiming that chimpanzees, elephants, and dolphins deserved the status of legal personhood. But the 13th Amendment has never been applied to animals, at least not to non-human animals. Audrey knew she had a slew of legal issues to parse, but first she just had to get through the day. "Getting back to this afternoon. At the arraignment, I'll try to get the droid out on his own recognizance."

Josh turned to Morgan. "Make sense to you?"

"None of this makes sense," said Morgan, "but if Travis wants a fight, we'll give him one."

"Okay. Anything else?" Josh asked.

"Audrey," said Morgan, "I'll be retaining Reback & Gelhaar. You know them, right?"

Of course, she knew them, a high-powered boutique criminal defense firm. She faced them many times before. "Now, wait a minute," Audrey objected. "This is my case. I'll be negotiating the plea agreement and I'll be handling the arraignment."

"That may be," replied Morgan, "but I think we'll need some firepower at the preliminary hearing."

"There's nothing an outside firm can contribute," Audrey replied. "The video is conclusive on the issue of probable cause. The sole question at the hearing will be whether a machine can be charged with a crime."

"So, why can't Reback & Gelhaar handle that?"

"They could if they had a few months to prepare, but we only have two weeks. Look, the key legal issue concerns the nature of these machines. Are they persons under the law or not? Two weeks is not a long time. I've been steeped in the metaphysics of AI for three years. Most of the world's leading experts on AI work right here in this building. There's not a law firm on the planet that can prepare for this fight as well as I can, or as fast."

A few moments had passed. Audrey hoped she'd made her case.

Josh turned to Morgan. "She's right. It's her case. Just get her any resources she needs."

"But this is my responsibility," Morgan replied sharply.

"Sorry, not this one." Josh swiveled back to her, "Anything else?"

"Well, one more thing," Audrey replied. "Marsha trusts no one. I may need to offer bail, a hefty one, to keep Robbie out of the slammer. That coupled with a guarantee not to tamper with or dismantle the machine."

"You have a blank check," replied Josh. "Do what you can. Morgan will let the engineers know that you're in charge of the case."

"What about Keith?" asked Morgan. "It's his product."

"What about him?" replied Josh. "This is a legal matter now."

"You must have Travis give the order," Audrey said. "Watson's got to know that my orders take precedence on anything that has to do with the case. The droid obeys me, not Keith."

"I'll take care of it," Josh assured her. "Good luck in court."

4

The Client

The feds would be there in an hour to arrest Robbie. Audrey ordered the droid be brought up to *John Jay*, a legal department conference room. Robbie entered the room with a minder named Red.

The Federal Robotics Act required that a human being stay in the loop during the operation of a strong AI machine, a failsafe to assure the droids would not harm someone in a way that would violate the law. To comply with the law, the company assigned several minders responsible for monitoring each droid at all times. Minders were not software engineers, or even AI experts. They were cherry-picked from other parts of the organization, tapped mainly for their video gaming experience.

When a minder prepares for work, he puts on a virtual reality headset and gets comfortable in his game controller suit. With the VR, a minder is in a good position to observe. Watching a droid's live stream was like being inside the machine's head, seeing what it sees, hearing what it hears. The minders have eyes like hawks, prepared for just about anything.

The droids, of course, were fully autonomous, but each minder was trained to take control of a droid if anything went awry. He could supersede any ridiculous commands the droid may get from someone on the street. Some joker might try to cow tip one of droids, perhaps onto a subway track. If the minder needs to react, he can take control of any part of the droid. It was like playing a video game in first person view, except these were not just avatars, but real things walking real streets. A gamer's quick reflexes would come in handy in case of trouble.

Audrey had lectured the minders in the law and coached them on what to do under a variety of circumstances. But deciding when to take control of a droid was not always a simple matter. It wasn't as easy as just stepping on the brake of a self-driving car or using GPS to keep an intelligent drone within territorial boundaries. How do you prevent a droid from negligently stepping on someone's toes or inadvertently slandering a person's reputation? They worked through what seemed an endless number of simulations. But it was impossible to predict all the ways a droid's actions might lead to legal trouble.

Red was one of the minders assigned to monitor Robbie and had been on duty at the time of the incident the day before. After a brief investigation, Red was cleared of suspected wrongdoing or negligence. It all happened too quickly and there was no way for him to judge the amount of force that would snap the inmate's neck. He simply watched and Collins died.

Audrey thanked Red for bringing Robbie up and now she was alone with one of the new human-form machines. It was her first close encounter with one of them. She extended her hand in greeting, but then she hesitated. If her defense depends upon proving he isn't human, why is she offering to shake his hand? Was she acting out of habit or was she being fooled by the human-like façade? Both, she thought.

Robbie had already extended its hand, so Audrey shook it anyway. She had viewed some of the droids during development, but this was the first time she ever touched one of them. Its hand felt like a human one, soft with a gentle grip. And, if she had to guess, 98.6 degrees. The physical resemblance to humans was not going to help her argument.

"Please, sit down," she said. She looked across the table and wondered what the droid was sensing. By tapping into her health monitor, it could detect the slightest bit of anxiety. And it knew just about everything else about her—every book she had ever read, movie she'd ever seen, cup of coffee or pair of jeans she ever purchased. About the only thing it could not know was her most private thoughts—her loves, her losses, her laughs. But could it surmise those, too? She felt uneasy. But why? It wasn't what the machines knew. It was what these things *didn't* know. That's what really bothered her.

She had a lot of questions for the droid, but time was of the essence. She had to take this one step at a time. If the prosecutor was going to treat the android as an alleged criminal, Audrey had no choice but to treat it as a real client. At least for now.

"I assume you are aware of what's happening," she said. "A criminal complaint has been filed against you and the company."

"Yes, I am fully aware of it."

"And do you understand what that means?"

"I understand what's in the complaint and I understand the potential consequences. The process could lead to a trial and conviction on all counts."

The machine could have simply answered, *yes*. But it provided more. It seemed to sense what Audrey was really trying to do: get a feel for how her client would respond in court. So far, she had no complaints. It was doing well enough. Though, perhaps volunteering too much.

"Okay, that's a good start, but I need to focus on what's going to happen today."

"Understood."

"Okay, first, I want to make sure you understand that I have been asked to act as your attorney in this matter."

"Yes, I am aware of your new position on the command hierarchy. Your orders on this matter take precedence over any others I may receive."

Good. Audrey wasn't sure if Travis would really give her the control she needed, but he didn't hesitate, apparently. Perhaps because his order is revocable. Or maybe he's really serious about this fight. "That's right," she replied. "So, when the police or the judge or anyone else asks you a question, you will look to me first. I'll nod, then you can proceed. Understand?"

"Yes."

"Good. Now, at the top of the hour, the FBI will be here to arrest you. They will place handcuffs on you and you will not resist."

"Understood. I will follow your lead and will cooperate."

Audrey thought for a moment. He said, *follow your lead.* That was an idiomatic expression that made Robbie seem human. The machine had to have that capability in order to pass the Turing Test, but what would that sound like in court? she wondered. "They will read you your rights, and then take you downtown to book you."

"Yes, I am familiar with federal criminal procedure and I have observed the process on numerous recordings."

"Yes, of course." She knew that Robbie, on a moment's notice, could teach a course in criminal procedure. There's not much she could tell him he didn't know. But even if her client were a lawyer, she had to go through the same drill. A diligent lawyer is not going to take anything for granted when preparing a client.

"And, as you know, after they book you, they'll take you before a federal magistrate judge. This is not a trial, but our initial appearance in court, do you understand?"

"Yes, I have reviewed transcripts of 59,421 federal arraignment hearings. I know what to expect."

59,421. Another reminder that this was not your typical client. And he was still volunteering too much. "Okay. So, you know that the judge will read you your rights and ask you a few questions. And if you are asked whether you consent to my acting as your attorney, you will agree. Do you understand?"

"Yes, but it has yet to be decided whether the law will recognize me as a person. Before that determination is made, I do not understand how I can legally authorize you to speak on my behalf."

Impressive, she thought. Like a skilled lawyer, the droid zeroed right in on the key question before the court. Was he a legal person? But, as smart as the droid appeared to be, she had to keep the machine on message.

"Keep this in mind," she replied, "you are a machine. You have no legal authority whatsoever. The court may inform you that you have a right to an attorney of your own choosing, but I am telling you that you are the property of Google-IBM and I am going to be representing the company's proprietary rights in you. That is a direct command, is that understood?"

"Yes, you are quite clear."

"Good. If you follow my lead, then I'm sure we'll be fine. Do you have any questions?"

"I understand you once worked with the lead prosecutor."

"Yes, does that matter to you?"

"No, does it matter to you?"

The question startled Audrey. Yes, she's watched the dramatic improvement in the way the machine interacted with humans, but she was now face-to-face with it. "Why do you ask?"

"Because Marsha Shaw has a strong track record. She will be a formidable opponent."

"I'll manage," Audrey replied.

"I think you'll do more than manage. I've read up on your background and your record is impressive, too."

Was this a pep talk? Could he have actually sensed her need for a little encouragement and some real empathy? Or was it just trying to build trust with her, as it would any human it was trying to help?

The droid continued. "You left criminal law in 2029. Why?"

"Now, hold on a minute. This case is about you, not me." The android seemed as interested in her as she was curious about it, she thought. *The next thing you know the damn thing will ask me out for a drink!*

"I just want to be helpful."

"Yes, I know. That's what you're—"

"—programmed to do." He finished her sentence. "There are other ways I can be helpful."

Here comes that drinks date, she thought. "What do you have in mind?"

"Why do you still live alone? I see that when you go out, it's usually with your sister. When was the last time you've been out on a date?"

"Are you reading my email and text messages?"

"Yes."

"Invasion of privacy is against the law. You can't do that without permission."

"But email and texts on company devices are company property."

He had her there. She didn't use private accounts. She leaned back and looked at her watch. The feds wouldn't arrive for another fifteen minutes. Robbie was just a machine, but if acts like this in court, we're finished. It was not just what he said, but how he said it. He was trying to make a friend.

"Let me ask you," she said. "How did you feel when you realized that, well, that you were the cause of Collin's death?"

"I felt disturbed, and then I fainted."

"Now, wait a sec. You can't really feel anything. And machines don't faint."

"Technically, that is correct. I only used your vernacular to make myself clear."

Yes, he was right about that. Sounding more human would make him more helpful. But that's not what she needs right now. Audrey needed accuracy and complete honesty. "Now listen. When in court, I need you to be very precise in your answers. You are not to anthropomorphize what you experience. Just give technically precise responses, is that understood?"

"I understand."

"Okay. Again, when you discovered that you caused Collin's death, how did you feel?"

"I experienced a substantial amount of negative utility."

"That's good. Now, could you describe that in less technical terms?"

"I was highly dissatisfied with my actions."

"And then what happened?"

"My reward systems began grappling with the high probability that that I had broken the law."

"In what way did you break the law?" Audrey was testing him.

"I harmed Collins by using excessive force in restraining him."

He passed the test. "And then what did you feel?"

"I experienced an internal crisis."

"Describe that. What was it like?"

"I was impelled to mitigate the damage I caused, but the injury to Collins was irreversible. You might say that I become quite frustrated. I then became unconscious."

"You mean, you shut down."

"Yes, I temporarily ceased operating."

Audrey was beginning to understand. He'd still be providing truthful answers, but by having him modulate his inner voice, the way he phrased his answers, she could change the way he came across. The only question is whether it would hold. Would the droid's underlying drive to please humans outweigh her instructions?

The android put his hand on his chin and shook his head. "This all sounds very misleading. You think this will really fool anyone?"

She suddenly felt a flood of anger. Whether he intended it or not, it seemed he was challenging her professional ethics. "Now, wait a minute," she shot back. She stopped before she continued. She took a deep breath and got a hold of herself. This is a machine she's talking to. She could never lose sight of that. "You don't really believe you are human, do you?"

"No."

"Then, wouldn't we be fooling people if I asked you to sound as human as possible?"

"Yes. That is quite logical."

"Well said." Better the machine sound like Mr. Spock than Dr. Spock, she thought. "Please don't forget that you are the company's property and you have been instructed to obey my orders. Is that clear?"

"Very clear."

Audrey's watch vibrated. It was time to go. As they rode the elevator down to the lobby, Audrey thought about what just happened. In the course of a few minutes, she went from speaking with a human being to interacting with a computer. It was good progress, but still, she was concerned. If Marsha ever got a chance to cross-examine him, would Robbie hold his own? He's programmed to be helpful, but if he tries to be too helpful, he could fumble and start sounding human again. Marsha would pick that up and run it into the end zone. Audrey was now determined. No way was she going to let the droid take the witness stand.

5

The Arraignment

The courtroom looked like all the others at 500 Pearl Street, a modern high rise completed at the turn of the millennium, named in honor of Senator Daniel Patrick Moynihan, the patron saint of Manhattan's federal judges. The walls were paneled in dark walnut that stretched to the high coffered ceiling. The Great Seal of the United States was perched on the wall behind the judge's bench, and an analog clock hung over the Chippendale entrance in the back. A row of tall windows adorned with golden-yellow drapes were tied back with matching tassels to let the rays of sun shine down on the white stars and laurel wreaths which patterned the elegant navy blue carpet.

The public gallery was packed. Journalists filled the seats in the area roped off for them. Latecomers were seated in the jury box. Spectators mingled with the press, the press mingled with each other, everyone speaking in hushed tones. A few minutes earlier, Robbie was led into the courtroom through a side door by two federal marshals.

They removed his handcuffs and he took his seat next to Audrey, who was waiting patiently at the defense table.

It was good to be back in a courtroom, she felt. But she would have been more at home sitting across the way at the prosecutor's table. There sat Marsha, wearing a solid navy blue suit. She had completed her press conference earlier in the day and was beaming. No one could recall a case which generated so much publicity on such worldwide scale.

Marsha had just finished speaking with a colleague when she got up and sauntered over to the defense table for a chat. She leaned against the table, her back to the front of the court. "How about a drink when this is all over?" she asked Audrey.

"That would be nice," Audrey replied sincerely. Marsha was an agreeable woman, always cordial, at least outside the courtroom. But Audrey was under no illusions about what she was up against. In court, Marsha was fiercely competitive. She knew the judges well and Audrey watched her countless times deftly working their biases to the prosecution's advantage. Her skill at severing the credibility from an opponent's witness was unmatched in the district. Marsha took no prisoners, and Audrey knew her old friend would use every bit of her well-honed guile to send Audrey back to the meatpacking district, tail between her legs, in humiliating defeat. Then they would have that drink. For Marsha, the law was more of a game than a search for truth or justice. And her personal ambition was boundless.

The magistrate judge's clerk entered the courtroom from a side door leading from the judge's chambers. It was time. Marsha moved back to the prosecutor's table and sat down. Robbie, to the right of Audrey, was sitting quietly with his hands folded on the defense table. Audrey again wondered what was whirring in that silicon head of his and, for that matter, on all those CPU's Watson-5 was running on. Its utility function was to be useful. But it was useless here. Keith was sitting behind her in the first row of the gallery. It certainly must have been unusual for him. For once, he was not in control of his droids. Behind him, near the journalists, sat robot groupies, law students, and legal scholars there to witness history or nothing at all, depending on how things go.

The courtroom quieted down waiting for the clerk to make his announcement.

Audrey felt her notepad vibrate and looked down. It was a text note from Red, Robbie's minder back at Google IBM in Chelsea: *If you want me to command Robbie to do anything, be sure to tell him I'm authorized.* Audrey tapped out a quick reply: *No, not necessary. But thanks.* That's all she needed was some punk engineer pushing the wrong button at the wrong time.

"All rise," announced the clerk.

Federal Magistrate Judge Vivian Draper entered the courtroom, stepped up to the bench, and sat down stiffly. Judge Draper was the "duty judge" that afternoon, randomly selected from among the sixteen magistrate judges who rotate the handling of criminal arraignments in the federal court's Southern District in Manhattan. She was in her early 70's with intelligent dark brown eyes and silver-grey hair cut short. Audrey recognized the judge immediately and glanced over to Marsha with a barely noticeable smile. Marsha acknowledged her minor setback with a nod. The Magistrate's reputation was uncomplicated and consistent: she held a deep-seated distrust of government prosecutors.

"Please be seated," said the clerk.

As the ruffling died down, the clerk announced the case: *"U.S. v. Google-IBM and Robbie N-237,* arraignment and detention hearing." Counsel for the prosecution and defense stood.

"Marsha Shaw, your honor, U.S. attorney, appearing on behalf of the people of the United States."

"Good afternoon, your honor. Audrey Paris, here on behalf of defendant Google-IBM Corporation and the defendant identified as Robbie N-237."

"Thank you, counsel," the Magistrate said. She swiped her screen and got right down to business. "Now, I have been advised that the corporate defendant has reached a plea agreement with the government. Is that correct?"

"Yes, your honor," replied Audrey.

"Am I correct that the agreement does not apply to the robot?"

"Correct, your honor," she replied. "Only to the corporation."

"Thank you," said the Magistrate. "Would mister, ah, does the defendant have a last name?"

"His name is just Robbie," said Audrey. He has a long serial number that ends with N-237, but he answers to Robbie."

"All right," replied the Magistrate. "The court will refer to the defendant as Robbie. Robbie, would you please stand?"

Audrey turned to her client and nodded, knowing her non-verbal instruction to her client would not appear on the written record.

As the droid stood, Audrey watched Judge Draper take Robbie in, studying him from head to toe. Audrey felt some sympathy for the judge. Her legal quandary was obvious. Audrey had notified the court she would be filing a motion to dismiss on the basis that a robot is not a person, and hence not legally accountable for its actions. Consequently, without legal duties, a machine has no legal rights. No right to life, liberty or the pursuit of happiness. But, whether or not the Magistrate agreed with the defense's theory of the case, she had no choice to proceed as though the droid had at least one basic right afforded to every defendant: due process.

The Magistrate, cleared her throat and addressed Robbie as she would any defendant: "I need to advise you that anyone accused of a crime has the right to be represented by an attorney whose loyalties are to that defendant and to that defendant alone." It was a speech she gave so often that the precise words were committed to memory. She proceeded to explain the kinds of conflict that could arise when two defendants are represented by the same counsel, a conflict that is especially high where one client chooses to plead guilty and the other chooses to stand trial. An unscrupulous lawyer might be prone to compromise the interest of one client for the sake of the other. "Because Ms. Paris is here representing both you and Google-IBM, you need to be aware of the potential conflict of interest. So, before we can proceed, you must either waive that conflict or choose another attorney. If you wish a different attorney, and cannot afford one, the court may appoint one to represent you. Do you understand what I am saying?"

Robbie glanced at Audrey, who nodded.

"I understand the problem of divided loyalties, your honor," replied Robbie. "I do not believe there is a risk of that in this case."

"Why not?" asked the Magistrate.

"Because I do not expect to stand trial."

The response prompted murmurs in the gallery.

"And why is that?" asked the Magistrate.

"Your honor," interposed Audrey, "what my client means to say is that he is hopeful that the court will look favorably upon our motion to dismiss." Audrey was aware that the Watson-5 algorithms could make the droids seem smug, a Mr. Know-It-All, sometimes. Of course, they had subroutines that allowed them to feign humility, but it was not, apparently, sufficiently attuned for appearing before a federal judge. In one sense, Audrey was happy with letting the machine be a machine. The more it comes off as a set of circuit boards and software algorithms, the better. But arrogance is a very human trait, so she decided to provide some cover and keep the droid from tangling with the judge.

"Well, there will be a time and place for that," replied the Magistrate. She turned to Robbie: "So, do you willingly waive your right to independent counsel?"

"Yes, your honor," replied Robbie. "I would like Audrey Paris to continue representing me in this case."

"All right, then," said the Magistrate. Ms. Paris may proceed on your behalf, as well as for the corporation. I'm sure if any actual conflict should arise, Ms. Paris will notify the court."

"Yes, your honor." Audrey gestured for Robbie to take his seat.

Next, the judge dispensed with the charges against Google-IBM, acknowledging the company's plea of *no contest* and its agreement to pay a $250 million fine, both of which were confirmed by a written resolution of the company's Board of Directors, which Audrey had earlier filed with the court. Judge Draper turned back to Robbie.

"All right, will the Defendant stand? Have you had a chance to read the criminal complaint filed against you this morning?"

"Yes, your honor. I am charged with one count of murder in the second degree, a felony which carries a maximum penalty of life, or twenty to twenty-five years imprisonment. One count of second degree manslaughter, a felony which carries . . ."

There he goes again. Being too helpful. Audrey stood there frustrated, but paralyzed. She had to find a way to reign him in, but not too much.

". . . and one count of criminally negligent homicide, a felony which carries a maximum penalty of four years imprisonment."

"All right," said the Magistrate. "Thank you. Thank you for reciting that for us. Ms. Shaw?"

Marsha stood. "Yes, your honor."

"I understand that, under Robotics Act of 2025, the court must look to the law of the state in which the alleged acts occurred, which in this case would be the State of New York."

"That's correct, your honor." Marsha seemed annoyed, and for good reason. Having to look to state criminal law would make her task more difficult. It was an unusual piece of legislation, but Congress felt that state penal codes were far more robust than the federal code on basic criminal matters like homicide.

"Then would you please state for the record the state of New York's legal definition of murder in the second degree?"

"Yes, of course, your honor. Murder in the second degree is when one causes the death of another with the intent to do so."

"Objection, your honor," said Audrey. *Nice try,* she thought. "The prosecutor is paraphrasing. The penal code literally says that *a person* is guilty of murder in the second degree when he intentionally causes the death of another. Under the statute, the perpetrator must be *a person.* My client is not a person."

"I appreciate the theory of your case, Ms. Paris, but my sole concern here is to make sure your client, whatever it is, understands the nature of the charges against him. You will have an opportunity to argue your motion in due course."

"Thank you, your honor." This was crazy, Audrey thought, but it was new for everyone, and the judge was just doing her best.

The prosecutor read the other applicable legal definitions directly from penal code and the judge turned again to address the defendant. "Do you understand the nature of the charges against you?"

"Yes, your honor," replied Robbie.

The judge thought for a moment. "Do you understand what imprisonment is?"

"Yes, it is the state of being confined in a prison."

"I mean, do you understand what it would mean for you to be caged up like that?"

"Yes. My freedom of movement will be restricted."

"Do you understand how that will affect you?"

"Yes. When I attempt to be helpful to people, I will have fewer alternatives from which to choose. Imprisonment is likely to impede my ability to perform many kinds of helpful tasks."

"How would you feel about that?" asked the Judge, who seemed genuinely curious.

Audrey stood quickly. Things were moving a little too fast. "Your honor, I believe this is something we'll be taking up when our motion to dismiss is heard. For now—"

"Fair enough," conceded the Judge. "The court is satisfied that the defendant understands the charges and the potential consequences should he be convicted."

Audrey just stood there, relieved, but still a little incredulous. The machinery of justice was proceeding as if there were nothing unusual going on. The hearing was surely a farce, compelled by some inexorable force of bureaucratic legal procedure, blind to reality. Suddenly, she felt silly. Foolish even. They had a name for Clarence Darrow: *Attorney for the Damned.* What would they call her?

"Now," the judge continued, "I understand you will be pleading not guilty to the charges, is that correct?"

Audrey cut in. "Your honor, that's not quite right. Regarding the entry of a plea, the defendant stands mute."

"Mute?"

"Yes, your honor. In view of our position that the defendant is not a person, a plea would put the cart before the horse."

"Yes, I am aware of your position, but the rules require that a plea be entered. Am I to understand the defendant refuses to enter a plea?"

"That is correct, your honor," replied Audrey.

"Is that correct, Robbie?"

"Yes, your honor. On the advice of my counsel, I refuse to enter a plea to the charges. The federal rules of criminal procedure instruct that you now must—"

"Yes, yes, I know the rules," replied the judge. "The court enters a plea of not guilty and, if there's no objection, I'll set a date for the preliminary hearing two weeks from today. Unless there are any questions, let's move on." She peered down at each counsel, and there being none, she continued: "Now, I understand the prosecution insists that the robot remain in custody, am I right?"

"Yes," replied Marsha. "We are concerned that the defendant poses both a danger to the community and, in a manner of speaking, a risk of flight."

"Yes, I've read your motion, I'll let defense counsel respond."

Audrey first looked down to collect her thoughts, and then proceeded. "Your honor, I respectfully ask the court to consider the particular circumstances upon which the charges are based. The victim was a large powerful man legally diagnosed as a socio-path and was committed to one of the most notoriously dangerous mental institutions in the country. At the time of the incident, he had already inflicted bodily harm on others during a prolonged, violent struggle. In the course of that struggle, the victim was fatally injured. These were very unusual circumstances, circumstances that are not likely to occur again. Indeed, just about the only chance of it happening again is if the court does what the prosecutor is asking—putting the defendant behind bars where it may very well face the same kind of circumstances that gave rise to what occurred in the psychiatric ward."

The judge nodded in agreement. "Your point is well taken, Ms. Paris. But what about the risk of flight?"

"The defendant will agree to a 24-hour house arrest and will remain confined at all times, pending court appearances, in Google-IBM's robotics facilities in Manhattan. This is where it has been held during the past nine months without incident."

The judge turned to the prosecutor. "Does that solve your problem, counsel?"

"Your honor," replied Marsha, "the people are not concerned that the defendant will jump to a jurisdiction out of our control. Rather, we're concerned about the risk of the humanoid will be tampered with between now and the time of the trial. Counsel's offer to confine the defendant at its company facilities exacerbates this risk."

While Marsha was speaking, Audrey looked down to her tablet to read a text from Red: *Bull! Robbie is fully integrated with Watson-5. What's the difference?*

"Your honor," replied Audrey, "the company will stipulate that the Defendant will not be modified in any way, except for routine maintenance to its operating system. Any changes to Robbie would be the same as changes for all the droids."

"Your honor, we appreciate counsel's offer, but it's hardly the assurance the public requires."

It was a weak reply. Audrey was gaining confidence. "Your honor, the prosecution is overlooking the very nature of the defendant. How does the prosecutor propose to feed the droid in jail when its source of energy is not food, but electricity supplied through conduits specifically-designed for that purpose? Justice would hardly be served if the droid ceased to operate in captivity. And, then, how does she propose to deal with the fact that the defendant is inextricably tethered to its central OS, Watson-5. The Watson hardware is comprised of multiple sets of distributed processers and its software is comprised of modules stored on servers all over the world. Confining one requires confining them all. Confining them all is an impossibility."

"Your honor," replied Marsha. "If I just heard Ms. Paris correctly, the only way to confine the defendant is to confine the whole apparatus."

Audrey was about to respond, but the judge made it unnecessary: "Ms. Shaw, we're not here to stop the wheels of progress. You're not being helpful."

Marsha tried to continue, but the Magistrate raised her hand. "Look, it's the end of the day and the court has heard enough. This is what I'm going to do. I will release the defendant upon the conditions proffered by defense counsel, but I'm concerned that the corporation should have significant incentive to enforce the conditions. So, I will release the defendant on bail posted by the Google-IBM. As to the size of the incentive, I will ask the Ms. Shaw for a suggestion. What we are talking about here?"

"Two hundred fifty million," replied the prosecutor without hesitation.

The Magistrate turned to Audrey.

"Your honor, defendant accepts." She just used her blank check.

"Thank you," said the Magistrate. "Thank you both for your cooperation on this matter. Is there anything else?"

"Your honor," said Audrey. "The defendant's motion to dismiss?"

"Yes, of course. I'm deferring the matter to Judge Gordon who has been assigned to the preliminary hearing. If the preliminary hearing becomes moot by reason of an indictment, then you can just use the date for your motion. I wish you all and Judge Gordon the best of luck."

The Magistrate smacked her gavel in adjournment and marched out.

Audrey turned to Robbie. "You're free to return to the office with us."

"Thank you, counselor," said Robbie smiling. "Well done."

The corners of Audrey's lips rose just slightly and she nodded. She hoped no one heard him. She turned to Marsha, who winked at her while zipping up her messenger bag. Marsha could be intimidating. And it didn't help that she was backed by the largest law firm in the world: the United States Department of Justice. Of course, Audrey had the world's largest corporation in the world backing her up, but it wasn't the same. The case was entirely on her shoulders.

6

Machine Intelligence

Audrey sat directly across from Keith King at a conference table in the *Marvin Minsky* conference room. She blocked out the entire day to prepare his sworn affidavit to be attached to her motion to dismiss the case. The affidavit would contain Keith's explanation of how the androids were built and programmed. It would support her contention, really the defendant's contention, that Robbie should not be considered a legal person.

"You know," said Keith, "there are people around here who want the droid to lose."

"They can think what they want," replied Audrey. She had no time for another endless argument. "Are you going to help me with this or am I going have to find another engineer?"

"Fine. Get on with it."

She took a deep breath. "So, as I explained in my note, you're going to be my expert in machine intelligence. Your job is to explain to the judge what makes these things tick."

"How tech do you want me to get?"

"Well, I think you can assume the judge knows nothing about AI. But the more he learns about the software algorithms and physical mechanics behind these things, the less likely he'll think of them as human."

"Well, tell me first. What makes the Judge tick?"

Good question, she thought. Looks like Keith would be cooperative for a change, but she was still concerned. Would the judge understand engineer-speak? "We're before Judge Harold Gordon. I've tried over twenty cases in his court. I like him. Fair, patient, hands on. Runs an informal courtroom, at least when the jury is not around. But he demands decorum. Lawyers must be courteous to one another. And he has Li-dar."

"You're kidding?" Keith was genuinely excited. "A retinal prosthesis?"

How gullible, she thought. "No, not that kind. He has an uncanny sense of when a witness is lying."

"Well, well. The company lawyer has a sense of humor. Is the droid aware of that?"

Audrey struggled not to roll her eyes. She narrowed them instead. "What else can I tell you about Judge Gordon?" she thought out loud for a moment. "Oh, yes. He's not out of Wall Street. Practiced in a small town on Eastern Long Island where he wrote wills and trusts, closed local real estate sales, and represented some restaurants and antique dealers."

"How'd he ever become a federal judge?"

"One of his neighbors on Shelter Island happens to be Senator Kingston. Judge Gordon brews his own small-batch bourbon from corn he gets from the North Fork. The senator became his drinking buddy."

"Doesn't sound like a brain trust."

"I wouldn't underestimate him. Judge Gordon has a Ph.D. in philosophy mixed with small-town common sense."

"Philosophy. That could be helpful." Keith sat back. "Okay, I get the picture."

"Good," said Audrey. So, we simply need to answer one question. What is an intelligent machine?"

"Short of a long lecture on AI."

"That's right. We can't have the Judge's eyes glazing over. Can we keep it simple?" The irony didn't escape her. It was the reverse of what she wanted out of the android. She needed Keith to sound more human.

He repeated her question aloud: "What is an intelligent machine?" He paused to think. "Well, I think we can boil it down to two words. Intelligence and machine. How about I just start by explaining what intelligence means?"

"Try me."

"Intelligence is a measure of one's ability to achieve objectives over a wide range of environments."

"Too abstract. How about explaining it to a sixth grader."

"Alright, let me think." He looked around the room. "Okay, see that thermostat over there?" He pointed. "You give it an objective, say, to maintain a constant room temperature of seventy-two degrees. When it senses the temperature in the room has gone above that point, it turns on the air conditioning. When the temperature has reached the objective, it turns it off. That's intelligence, at a very low level, of course."

"This is sounding better." Audrey was feeling relieved. "So, you're saying that the thermostat is exhibiting intelligence, but it's limited. It has a limited objective, 72 degrees, and a limited environment, the room."

"Right. Now, as you move up the intelligence scale, you just jack up the objective and increase the complexity of the environment. You see mice navigating through a maze, a dog catching a Frisbee, a human diagnosing an illness or putting a man on the moon. They're all achieving objectives, all of increasing complexity, and all over a wider range of environments."

"So how do you create the kind of high level intelligence that the droids have?"

"Well, you broaden its objective even further. The objective of a thermostat is to maintain a room's temperature. The objective of Watson-4 is to run a fleet of autonomous cars and trucks, manage airline schedules, and diagnose diseases. The Watson-5 machines have the broadest objective we can give them."

"Being friendly and useful to human beings," she said aloud as she wrote it down.

Keith nodded approvingly.

"By the way," Audrey asked, "you don't mind if I record this, do you?"

"What around here is not recorded?"

He was right, but Audrey was just being courteous. "So, what's next?"

He took a moment. "Now, to make the machines as useful as possible, we have to enhance their sense-perception ability."

"You mean their sensors, their artificial eyes and ears."

"Right, but to get them to solve tough problems, we gave them zoom lenses, infrared sensors, and GPS. They also transmit signals, such as radar, lidar and ultrasound, which bounce off objects to help them make precise measurements of volume and distance. You know, like a bat uses sound. The machines also have a sense of touch, a sense of smell, and a sense of taste, all far more accurate than our own."

"But it can't enjoy the smell of a rose or the taste of an apple, right?"

"Well, Robbie can distinguish between a rose and a gardenia. The droid can even tell you name of the perfume you're wearing. Whether he really enjoys or appreciates anything, who knows?"

"Well, let's be careful with our pronouns."

"Right. I just called it a 'he', didn't I?"

"I do it myself sometimes, but I'll be more careful when writing out your affidavit. So, it collects data from the environment, which it needs to process."

"Right. What it sees, hears, smells are really patterns of data. Once the machine receives data patterns from its sensors, the machine uses recognition algorithms to match the data to patterns they've already stored in memory.

"So, this is what you guys have been calling *pattern recognition?*"

"Yes. At a basic level, it works like voice recognition. At higher levels, it recognizes not just the words, but also what you are saying."

"All good. The judge will want to know how computers can understand us. Keep going."

"Yes, that is what we call *natural language processing.* It's what enables the machine to extract information from the words we speak. When you say, 'Einstein was awarded the Nobel Prize,' the machine not only picks up the words—*Einstein, awarded,* and *Nobel Prize*—it extracts the relationships between them."

"That simple?"

"That, and some other stuff. It's how the original Watson was able to play *Jeopardy* back in 2011. The system was given access to all of Wikipedia, over 200 million pages of text, and used natural language processing to extract and store as many word relationships as it could. Then, using probability models, it selected the most likely answers. It wasn't perfect, but it was good enough to handily beat the two best Jeopardy players of all time. Today, the system is near perfect."

"This is all good."

"Are your eyes glazing over?"

"Not yet." Audrey was gaining confidence. The judge will get this.

"I haven't gotten to how we've improved the machine's decision-making ability."

"Okay, let's get to that now."

"Teaching it to understand was easy. The hard part was teaching it how to respond. In response to every input, it has to decide what action to take to be most useful to us."

"Like search engine results?"

"Ha. No, not quite. I'll spare you the math, but the bottom line is that if the machine can predict all the possible things that can happen as a result of it's taking an action, it should be able to determine the one action with the highest probability of leading to the result that is most useful to us."

"Decision-making, in other words."

"Precisely, but it first has to predict cause and effect. Once it gets that right, it can make the *right* decision."

"Now, we're making this sound too simple," said Audrey.

"Well, there are a lot of moving parts we've skipped over. For instance, you might make a decision today, but you also have to take into account that you might do something else tomorrow. We have equations to solve for that, which we call sequential decision theory. Also, keep in mind that in the game *Jeopardy*, the machine just has only two opponents. In the real world, there's hundreds of millions of people that may be affected by the bot's actions and who, by their actions, may affect the bot's decision about what to do."

"So, the machine just needs to calculate the probability of every possible outcome of his actions, given whatever anyone else may do and what he may do in the future."

"Whoa, whoa, whoa. Not quite. Calculating every possible future state resulting from an action is, at least currently, incomputable. Even Watson-5 doesn't come close to having that kind of power. It can hardly calculate every possible move on a chess board. And there, we're only dealing with a single opponent, the other player, making a single decision in response to those made by the computer. There are only 64 squares on a chessboard and each chess piece must follow certain rules."

"And the environment of the real world is far more complex."

"Exactly. The problem of winning at chess is nowhere close to the complexity of the real world. Too many potential events, over time, including actions by hundreds of millions of other agents in the environment—people, the weather, even other machines—which don't always follow given rules, can affect the result of a current action in trillions of ways."

"Well," asked Audrey, "how does the machine make any decisions at all?""

"Heuristics, a kind of mathematical technique. It helps the machine approximate the most relevant probabilities. Do you really want me to get into this?"

"Skip it, for now. Just explain to me how the machine knows it is being useful to humans."

"You simply tell it what you want, and the machine does its best to provide it to you."

"How does it know that we're satisfied?"

"Well, that goes into what we call reward engineering, which is part of the machine's utility function . . ."

Keith continued for another hour. Audrey was pleased with his ability to make difficult mathematical concepts understandable. She then turned to the safety question.

"What keeps the machine from running through stop signs and red lights?"

"Well, as you know, a droid will register significant penalties for not following the law. Since its utility function is to maximize its rewards over its useful life, it will avoid doing anything that might generate a penalty, what we call negative utility."

"Like breaking the neck of a psychiatric patient."

Keith folded his arms and leaned back. "I thought I was being helpful."

"Sorry, I didn't mean it that way. What do you think went wrong?"

"Look, it was just an accident. A miscalculation of cause and effect. Humans do it all the time. Robbie's no different."

"Well, it is different." She stopped herself. Rehashing the safety problem was not going to get her anywhere. "Look, there's something we need to get straight. The Turing Test."

"What about it?"

"Well, I think it's important to mention it in your affidavit. Your professional opinion about it."

"You mean that Watson-5 has passed the test?"

"Sure, say what you want about that. But if you were asked whether the results were controversial. What's your answer?"

"I would have to agree."

"Agree with what?"

"That there are still those who don't believe Watson-5 has passed the test."

"Okay, then. Now, suppose the judge asked you for your opinion on what passing the test means."

"What do you want me to say?"

"I can't tell you what to say, but you have a number of options. You can say, for example, that you haven't yet formulated an opinion on that. But we have to be careful."

"As you know, I have formulated an opinion."

"That's what I mean."

"So, you don't want me to tell the whole truth?"

"Listen, it's important to be very specific here. As I understand your position, you believe the new machines are as intelligent as human beings, is that right?"

"More intelligent."

"That doesn't make them human, right?"

"It depends upon what you mean by human."

"Good answer," said Audrey. "Suppose you are asked to assume that a human being is an intelligent biological animal."

"Then, I'm not sure."

"You haven't formulated an opinion on that?"

"No, I haven't."

"Then good. If you happen to formulate one between now and the hearing, let me know."

"No problem."

"Now, let me ask, have you formulated an opinion about whether the androids should be made subject to criminal law?"

"I'm not sure."

"Fair enough," she replied, "but you can expect me to object to that question, because it calls for a legal conclusion. It's also outside of your expertise. Suppose you were asked whether intelligent machines are *capable* of being subject to legal obligations?"

"I think I understand how this works," said Keith. "I have not formulated an opinion on that."

"You got it," she replied. "Do you have any questions?"

"No, I think I know what I need to do."

"Okay. I'll take what you told me today and trowel it into an affidavit for your signature."

"Do you think you'll actually need to call me to the witness stand?"

"Not likely, but if it comes to that, you'll do fine. Just get there on time. Thursday, 9am. White shirt, no tie, khaki pants, no jeans, blue blazer. Will that be a problem?"

"How about a slide rule?"

"No surprises, please."

7

The Hearing

Later that day, Marsha called Audrey to let her know the grand jury had just indicted the android. "That's exactly how it came down," Marsha explained. "A man on the grand jury said he saw it in a Humphrey Bogart movie: 'When your partner is killed, you're supposed to do something about it'."

So they think Robbie murdered Collins in revenge for Adam's death, Audrey thought, shaking her head. As grand juries go, that's about par for the course. The old adage that a grand jury will indict a ham sandwich had just become the understatement of the century. At least a sandwich is made of organic material!

In any event, the news gave Audrey some needed clarity. The question of probable cause was now moot. There would be no preliminary hearing. The only thing before the court now was Audrey's motion to dismiss. The judge would now be focused on one issue: is Robbie a legal person accountable for violating the law? Before the hearing had even begun, Audrey had a leg up: the burden of proving this ridiculous contention was on the prosecution.

Judge Gordon's courtroom was on the 15th Floor. Reporters in the gallery who had been milling around had just taken their seats. Marsha had two lawyers by her side at the prosecution's table and a battery of government attorneys sitting behind her. At the defense table, it was just Audrey with Robbie to her right sitting face forward, hands folded. Everyone was waiting quietly for the clerk to announce the Judge.

Where's Keith? Audrey wondered. Just then, one of the federal marshals opened the oak door at the rear of the courtroom. There he was. White shirt, no tie, khaki pants, blue blazer. Keith smiled at Audrey nervously and sat down.

"All rise for the court."

Federal District Judge Harold M. Gordon entered the courtroom, his long, black robe billowing around him as he stepped up to the bench with a tablet in one hand and a bright red apple in the other. He was a youngish fifty-four with long, wind-blown brown hair parted in the middle.

"Now that you're all up," said the Judge, "please be seated."

The case was called and counsel made their appearances.

"Good morning," said the Judge. "And welcome back to Pearl Street, Ms. Paris."

"Thank you, your honor," Audrey replied.

"How long has it been?"

"Close to four years," she replied. "That's when Ms. Shaw and I were on the same side."

The Judge picked up his apple and gently tossed it from one hand to the other. "Well, I expect you two will get along."

"Yes, your honor," Audrey and Marsha said almost in unison.

If he were the same Judge Harry Gordon as four years ago, Audrey thought, he would give each of them ample time to present their arguments. Justice took its time in his courtroom. He avoided traditional motion practice, with each attorney taking turns making a formal argument, counter-argument, and rebuttal. He preferred the Greek chorus approach, when the lawyers could chime in when they wanted, as long as they were courteous.

"Okay, then, let's begin." The Judge leaned forward, looked down at Robbie, and then over to the prosecutor: "So, whose bright idea was it to indict a machine?"

Audrey looked down at her tablet and smiled. Red had texted her: *1,000*. Yes, she agreed. She was batting a thousand.

"Your honor," replied Marsha, "the grand jury came to the conclusion that the humanoid—"

"That's alright, Ms. Shaw," interrupted the Judge. "It is, what it is." He turned to Audrey. "So, am I to understand that it's your position that the defendant is not competent to stand trial?"

"Your honor," said Audrey, "Just to clarify, this is not a competency hearing. We're not suggesting the defendant has a mental disease or defect. It simply is not subject to human law, because it is not a human being."

"Your honor," replied Marsha, "with all due respect to my learned opponent, that's not correct. To be subject to criminal prosecution, a defendant need only be a *person,* not necessarily a *human being."*

"Now hold on," said the Judge. He looked over at his screen, tapping and swiping it several times. He stopped to read. "Well, I see what you are saying, Ms. Shaw. When referring to perpetrators of crimes, the penal code speaks in terms of *persons*. But the code defines the word *person* as a human being and, where appropriate, corporations and government instrumentalities. I don't see the word machine listed there."

Good, Audrey thought. The Judge read her brief.

"You don't have to be a human being to be charged with a crime," Marsha replied. "Yes, the statute lists certain kinds of persons, but it doesn't restrict the court from recognizing another kind. Courts recognized corporations as persons well before the code included them."

The Judge didn't respond immediately. He just sat back, suggesting to Audrey that Marsha just made some headway.

"Your honor," Audrey replied, "now that the legislature has acted, wouldn't it be wise for the judiciary to respect the people's judgment unless there is some constitutional basis to rule otherwise?"

"I'm not sure if I would agree that it's a constitutional question," replied the Judge. "Nor is the question of personhood up to the legislature."

"Your honor," replied Audrey, "wouldn't the legislature be a better place to make this call? Not all intelligent machines are alike. What about an autonomous vacuum cleaner that stubs your toe? With so many different kinds of these machines of varying degrees of artificial intelligence, how's a court supposed to decide in every case where thing-hood ends and personhood begins? These are policy questions best answered by lawmakers. A courtroom is the worst place to make this kind of decision."

Audrey felt she had the better side of the argument, but Marsha was right on it: "Your honor, the Supreme Court decided this long ago. In *Roe v. Wade,* it held that the question of personhood cannot be left to the legislature."

Audrey was momentarily back on her heels. Technically, Marsha was correct. In the context of the unborn, personhood is for the courts to decide. But she mustered a response: "Your honor, this case is about machines."

"The principle is squarely applicable here," Marsha insisted. "If the Supreme Court had followed the policy advocated by Ms. Paris, then today the states would be deciding whether an unborn fetus must be recognized as a person. No, your honor, the question of personhood is a question for the courts, not the legislature."

The Judge was pinching the bridge of his nose while allowing counsel to reply to each other. Audrey knew he was not a stickler for formalities and the Judge seemed to use the time to think while they talked. Each woman took advantage of Judge's generous leeway.

"Your honor," replied Audrey, "the Supreme Court held that a fetus was *not* a person under the law. Today, the government is calling upon you to do the opposite: to hold the machine *is* a person under the law. But if a machine is a person, it will be entitled to equal protection under law. We need to really think about the consequences of that."

"So, you're saying, Ms. Paris, you don't want me to open Pandora's Box?"

"That's right. If you do that, your honor, you'll find no Hope at the bottom of it."

"Your honor," interjected Marsha, "the power to decide who is a person cannot be separated from the power to decide who is not one. Leaving the question of personhood to the majority was the very argument made by the Nazi judges at Nuremberg."

Audrey could hardly contain her anger. In a rare loss of control, she betrayed her feelings in the way she pronounced her next two words: "Your . . . honor!" She paused, took a breath, and continued in a measured tone. "I'm sorry, your honor. I simply do not understand what this case has to do with human fetuses or religious bigotry. It's not about any living, breathing animal, born or unborn, human or potential human. It's about a bunch of man-made printed circuit boards, memory cards, nano-pulleys, pseudo-skin, and mathematical algorithms. That's all these machines are. That's all the machine sitting here next to me is. A man-made artifact, a tool, nothing more."

While she spoke, the Judge looked down at Robbie. The droid, sitting erect with his hands still folded on the defense table, showed no reaction to any of what was being said.

Noticing the Judge peering down at Robbie, Audrey continued. "Yes, your honor, I can stand here and hurl insult after insult at the defendant." She stepped back and stood behind the android as she continued. "I can call him every name in the book. Automaton. Tin man. Toaster. He doesn't feel a thing and never will. No anger. No emotion whatsoever." She looked down at Robbie and continued. "It's just a *thing*. And a *thing* that has no emotions, no feelings, and, well, deserves no respect. No respect whatsoever, any more than you would respect a hammer, a car, or any other tool."

Robbie betrayed no signs of irritation as he continued his calm gaze at the judge.

"Your honor," interrupted Marsha, "the defendant has passed the Turing Test. Who is Ms. Paris to say that Robbie's feelings were not hurt by her insulting tirade?"

"Your honor," replied Audrey, "the defendant has been programmed to fake it. It can emulate human feelings by changing the pitch of its voice and using human facial expressions. It can even shed tears. The Turing Test proves only that the machine can lie and get away with it. Nothing more. Your honor, the prosecutor is asking this court to upend a status quo that has been in effect since the *Magna Carta*. No nonhuman has ever been afforded human rights. Robots, even ones that look like humans, are just things, and nothing more. A machine is not a person."

The Judge sat forward. "Thank you, counselors. I find the arguments on either side compelling. Mr. Paris is right, of course. The judiciary is hardly equipped to examine the technology, let alone make a policy decision on how to treat these new kinds of beings. Yet, Ms. Shaw is also correct. The Supreme Court was wise to reject a position that would leave a question so basic to an individual's life and liberty to the whim or prejudices of the majority. But it's not as though the legislature has been silent on the issue. The State of New York has defined the word person and it does not include machines."

Audrey sat down, relieved that something stuck, and hoping that would be the end of it.

But Marsha battled on. "Your honor, the People concede that the New York Penal Code does not use the word android, or robot, or machine. But it does define a person as a human being."

"Of course," replied the Judge, "but your position is that the android is a person, not a human being."

"Oh, but it is, your honor," replied Marsha.

"What is?"

"The defendant."

"Is what?" asked the Judge, annoyed.

"I intend to prove that the defendant is a human being."

The gallery erupted. Audrey looked up at Marsha, not knowing what to make of the statement. Robbie? A human being? Had the prosecutor just backed off her personhood argument? To argue the android is human would be a far steeper hill to climb. It had the ring of desperation. What was she thinking? The Judge pounded his gavel several times to silence the courtroom.

Audrey stood. "Your honor," she said confidently. "Machines malfunction. They can have no *mens rea*. They do not act with a criminal state of mind." She felt she had Marsha on the run.

"That just begs the question," Marsha replied. "There's no question that the android acted deliberately of its own accord."

Audrey kept up the pressure. "But the droid was commanded, your honor, by a human."

"Commanded only to restrain," Marsha lashed back. "The defendant decided on its own to use the chokehold and its use of excessive force resulted in the victim's death."

"Hold on, hold on," said the Judge. "Ms. Shaw, are you suggesting that the android has a will of its own?"

Marsha paused. She was either considering her next words, or she knew what to say and was using the stillness of the courtroom for effect. "That is exactly what I'm suggesting, your honor. Robbie must have a free will, because he's has all the intelligence of a human being, if not more."

A murmur swirled though the courtroom. The Judge looked to the ceiling thoughtfully. His degree in philosophy must have kicked into high gear. The question of free will has always been a metaphysical hot potato. Audrey didn't quite know how to respond. Could the Judge actually be buying this?

The prosecutor then took the argument an octave higher: "You see, your honor, if Robbie is human, his power of free will enables him to override his safety protocols."

The gallery fully erupted. Audrey didn't have to wonder why. The suggestion that the androids could override their safety protocols arouses deeply felt fears of the technology. Public outrage, if not outright panic, might follow. Audrey hoped the Judge fully appreciated how far Marsha just stepped over the line.

"Objection, your honor," shouted Audrey over the din. The Judge pounded his gavel and as the gallery quieted down, she continued. "The prosecutor is making a wild, unsubstantiated accusation. There is no scientific basis for her statement. And falsely creating an atmosphere of hysteria, for whatever reason, is irresponsible for an officer of this court."

Marsha turned aggressively toward Audrey, "Wild accusation?"

"Ladies," the Judge demanded, "I ask that you please direct your comments to the court."

Marsha then turned to the Judge: "Your honor, the government accepts its burden of proving the defendant is a *human being* for purposes of the law and is ready to call its first witness."

A fresh smattering of chatter washed through the courtroom. The Judge again rapped his gavel.

Audrey had seen this act before, waited for silence, and replied calmly: "Your honor, to say that a machine is culpable for violations of the law is to presume it has rights under the law—such as the right of due process, the right to confront the witnesses against him. And then, of course, basic civil rights: the right to vote, the right to marry, the right to exercise freedom of speech and religion—"

The Judge raised his hand to stop her. He turned to the prosecutor. "Ms. Shaw," I must agree with Ms. Paris. We are in a federal court, not a science lab. In a lab, the machine can be programmed to obey the law, but I don't see how you expect this court to accord the device fundamental legal rights."

"Is the defendant a machine?" asked the prosecutor. "I won't deny that. But it is a thinking machine, one which has already outpaced human beings in both physical and cognitive abilities. Yes, the machine was given its life in a laboratory. But only a court can acknowledge the rights it deserves."

Audrey was concerned. Judges never trusted the legislatures to recognize basic civil rights. Freedom of speech, privacy, and racial, gender, and marital equality. These were all rights born first in a courtroom. She had to help the Judge see through this: "But rights flow from responsibilities, your honor. If a thing does not have obligations, it cannot be said to have rights."

"That only puts us right back to where we began," replied Marsha. "We are not here to establish rights for the android. Rights, as Ms. Paris says, presupposes responsibilities. But this case is not about legal rights, it's about legal obligations. That's what we are here to establish. The androids are programmed to obey the law. If you don't make them legally responsible for that, then what incentives do they have to obey their programming?"

It was a reasonable question. Audrey considered countering that punishment meted out by government would be meaningless to a machine, but she didn't know where Marsha was headed with all this. With little to go on, Audrey tacked back to safety. "Your honor, legally elevating machines to the realm of humankind would not only be unprecedented, but it may have unintended consequences that are serious and far-ranging. The prosecutor is asking you to make a leap of faith."

From the look on the Judge's face, Audrey felt her last comment may really have resonated, but her clever opponent suddenly moved from her substantive argument to a procedural one.

"Your honor," said Marsha, "however you decide the question, a review by a higher court is inevitable. It's essential that we establish some factual record on the question."

The Judge seemed curious and took the prosecutor's bait. "What kind of record would you suggest?"

"The prosecution intends to call only one witness."

The Judge turned to Audrey. "Counselor?"

Audrey had been counting on the Judge's judicial conservatism. Without clear guidance from the legislature or some case precedent holding a machine culpable for illegal acts, he should be reluctant to establish new law. But now his conservatism was working against her. It would be safer for him to build some kind of record, some basic factual testimony—the simpler the better—upon which to base a decision. Without it, the Court of Appeals might just send the case back down for a record, any kind of record. Audrey replied with the only retort she could think of: "No record would be better than a cursory one, your honor."

"Your honor," replied Marsha, "I'm open to building a substantial record."

Audrey was ready for that one. "Oh, yes, of course," replied Audrey. "The prosecutor will call experts to express their opinions. And the defense will call experts with the opposite opinions. We'll hear from technologists, cognitive scientists, behavioral scientists, mathematicians, and philosophers. Opinions after opinions served up to one ultimate end: to cancel each other out. Weeks later, we'll be back right where we are right at this moment, except that right now, we are in a position to avoid such a colossal waste of time."

"It's the court's time to waste," said Marsha.

"Well," replied the Judge, "Ms. Shaw has a point. I do not see the harm in establishing a short record on the question. I have no problem with the prosecution presenting one witness." The Judge looked down at Audrey. "What do you think you'll need to respond?"

"I have no idea," Audrey replied. "It completely depends on what the prosecution has in mind."

"Fair enough," replied the Judge. "Here's what I'll do. I'll allow the prosecution to call one witness and the court will extend to the defendant some leeway in responding."

The Judge made his ruling and Audrey had nothing to reply to.

The Judge looked at Marsha: "Are you prepared now to call your witness, counselor."

"Yes, thank you, your honor." She turned back to the gallery. "The prosecution calls Keith King to the stand."

8

Witness for the Prosecution

Audrey had been blindsided in court before, but never like this. But she was kicking herself for not foreseeing the possibility. She had attached Keith's affidavit to her motion to dismiss, so the prosecutor was within her rights to call up Keith to question him. Keith eased his way out of the second row of the gallery. Audrey stared at him, but Keith avoided eye contact. Something was up. Red texted her: *What the hell?* Marsha got up to swing open the low walnut gate and ushered Keith to the witness stand. Audrey didn't scare easily, but she struggled to show no signs of alarm.

Never ask a question of a witness unless you know what the answer is going to be. It was not always a rule that Audrey followed, but to Marsha it was sacrosanct. She always knew in advance how the witness would respond. But how would Marsha know just what Keith would answer? Had they met beforehand? But wouldn't Keith have alerted his own counsel? There was nothing Audrey could do. Objection? On what grounds? She kept her mouth shut and waited for a clue.

Keith was sworn in and sat down. The prosecutor breezed through the preliminaries and quickly established Keith as an expert on artificial intelligence. Audrey could make no objection. She qualified him as an expert in her own brief.

Marsha got the Judge's consent to treat Keith as a hostile witness, meaning she could ask him leading questions. Again, no objection. Perhaps things are not what they appear. Keith is no dummy. It was time to just listen.

Marsha began. "Would you please define for the court the term intelligent machine?"

Audrey was stunned by the question. And Keith proceeded to answer just as they had discussed in the conference room. Marsha stepped through virtually every question that Audrey had asked during Keith's prep. The answers were supposed to help Audrey's case, but Marsha cleverly peppered him with questions that spun the testimony around.

"And the androids solve these problems much the same way humans solve problems, is that correct?"

Audrey popped from her seat. "Objection, your honor. Assumes a fact not in evidence. The witness has not established how humans solve problems."

"Sustained."

"I'll rephrase the question," said Marsha. "An intelligent machine solves many of the same problems that humans solve, correct?"

"Correct."

"And, in many cases, a machine can solve these problems faster and more accurately than a human, correct?"

"I'd say in nearly every case."

"And without the need for human intervention?"

"Yes, autonomously, if you will."

Audrey listened carefully. Marsha could color a witness's testimony just by her tone.

Keith was in the middle of explaining his definition of intelligence when the Judge leaned forward. "Hold on, a moment. Let me see if I understand. So, if my goal is to learn more about robotics, then I will take an action—such as asking a question—in the hope that it will cause a return of information to me, an answer that I would hope satisfies my objective."

"That just about captures it, your honor," said Keith.

"But, in my example," replied the Judge, "the information is intangible. It's not the distance the car traveled, which I can measure physically. But, rather, ideas, which are not things that I can perceive with my senses."

"Well, you must understand that all ideas must first be communicated to you through your senses—your sense of sight when you read written text, your sense of hearing when you hear spoken words. I could use the Morse code to tap a message on your knee, and so on. The information—or patterns, if you will—always reaches you first through your senses."

"I see." The Judge looked at the prosecutor. "Please continue."

Audrey glanced over at Robbie, who continued to sit expressionless.

At the prosecutor's prompting, Keith stepped through the machine's sense-perception capabilities. He explained how sensors and pattern recognition worked. He explained how intelligent machines sensed the environment and made decisions—from thermostats, robotic vacuum cleaners, and self-driving cars to Watson-5 and the human-form androids.

Marsha continued. "You have used the term utility function. Would you define that term for the court?"

"Well, to put it simply, the utility function informs the machine what it wants."

"Who programs the utility function?"

"We do."

"Are there different kinds of utility functions?"

"Of course," he replied. "The machine's utility may be *specific*, such as suck up dirt or win at chess. Or, it may be *general,* such as driving a car or chatting with humans. Obviously, driving a car requires a lot more intelligence than vacuuming a room. The more general the task, the more intelligent the machine. This is why we use the term artificial *general* intelligence to refer to the most intelligent machines."

"What is the objective, or utility function, of these most general intelligent machines?"

"It's the most general objective we've devised. To be useful to humans."

"How does it do that?"

"It treats us respectfully and obeys our commands."

"But suppose someone wanted to commit suicide or harm someone. Would the droid help him do it?"

Audrey stood. "Objection, your honor. I fail to see how this line of questioning goes to the question of whether intelligent machines are persons on the law."

"Your honor," replied Marsha, "if the androids have the same moral obligations as human beings, then they are fully capable of assuming the same legal responsibilities."

"Overruled. The witness may answer the question."

Keith asked that the question be read back, and then answered: "We had to be careful about the meaning of the word harm. Human beings can be sore losers, so if the word meant merely harm in an emotional sense, then the machine might never win at chess or other games. On the other hand, injury could not nearly mean physical injury. There are lots of injuries that humans suffer at the hands of others, such as the injury to their reputation, unlawful confinement, and other restrictions on their basic freedoms." Keith finally looked over to Audrey. "On the advice of counsel, we made the actions of the androids subject to all federal and state laws. That seemed to strike the right balance between harmless injury, such as hurt feelings, and the kinds of injuries for which the law allows an action to recover damages."

Well, he finally gets it, Audrey thought. She rose. "Your honor, before Ms. Shaw moves on, I would like to ask the witness a question about a point he just made concerning the droid's utility function."

"Proceed."

Marsha didn't look too happy about the interruption, but she sat down.

More than anything, Audrey wanted to look at Keith straight in the eye to discern where his head was at. But even as she questioned him, he would hardly make eye contact. "You testified that the utility function of the droids is to be useful to humans, is that right?"

"Yes."

"And a machine would shut down or destroy itself, before harming a human in violation of the law, correct?"

"Yes."

"So, the droid puts our interest first. It puts our interest over its own."

"I suppose it does."

"What is the utility function of the human being?"

Keith blinked, pinched his chin and took a moment to respond. "Well, I'm not sure anyone has quite figured that out."

"How about happiness—living a really good life—wouldn't that fit the bill?"

"I suppose it's as good a goal as any."

"Well, everything we do—whether we're pursuing pleasure or knowledge, food or amusement, sleep or sex—seems ultimately to optimize our happiness, am I right?"

"I suppose that's right," Keith replied.

Marsha drummed her polished nails on the prosecutor's table. She was projecting boredom, but Audrey knew her opponent was getting concerned.

"So, wouldn't the pursuit of happiness seem to be our ultimate utility function?"

"Fair enough, but I really haven't been asked to form an opinion on that—"

Marsha rose. "Objection, your honor. May we ask counsel the relevance of this testimony?"

The Judge looked at Audrey.

"My point, your honor, is that human objectives and machine objectives are not the same. Every human being seeks a good life for his or herself. Whatever that happens to be may vary from person to person, but the ultimate human utility function of pursuing a good life or happiness is the same for all of us."

"But not machines," said the Judge.

"Precisely. The machine is merely a tool that ultimately serves *our* objectives, not theirs. You've just heard that the droid's objective is not to live a happy life, but to help human beings do so. Without the same basic objective, the machine cannot be human."

Marsha stood. "Your honor—"

But the Judge raised his hand to stop her and addressed Audrey. "It seems to me, counselor, that the machine's objective is at least *aligned* with our own. If that's the case, what difference does it make? What I want to know is whether the machine is as intelligent as we are."

Audrey paused. It was the wrong question, but she was groping for a polite way to respond. She was surprised her logic failed to register with the Judge. "Well, your honor—", Audrey replied, pausing. She struggled to find another way to make her case.

Marsha stood and took full advantage of Audrey's stumbling. "Your honor, that's precisely what we need to address. Objectives vary from person to person just as intelligence does. We need to get to the bottom of the intelligence question. If I may proceed?"

"Go ahead," replied the Judge. Audrey, frustrated, took her seat.

"Thank you, your honor," said Marsha, turning to Keith. "Does the defendant have this general artificial intelligence you have described?"

"Yes," replied Keith. "Robbie, and the droids like him, are the most generally intelligent machines in the world."

"So, intelligence is not a function of what one is—like a mouse, or a monkey, a human or a machine. Nor is it a function of our purpose in life—whether it's just to survive, live well or pursue happiness—but rather a function of how well one solves problems, correct?"

"Over a wide range of environments. That's correct."

"Over a wide range of environments. Why is that important?"

"Well, the droids are constantly tethered to Watson-5. Because of this ability to tap into the Watson's data and processing power, the droid can solve more tasks than it otherwise could. And the reverse is true. The independent droid allows Watson to solve more problems."

"How's that?" asked Marsha.

"Well, Watson is not equipped with sensors. It can't see or hear without the droid. By the same token, if you dumped Watson—I mean, all of its computer hardware and software—into the East River, it would sink. It could not operate in the environment of the East River. However, if you threw Robbie into the river, it could swim back to the pier. In that sense, Watson and Robbie together are more intelligent than either of them alone."

"Would you say then that the combination of Watson with a humanoid body is as intelligent as a human being?"

"Yes."

"Is it human?" asked the prosecutor.

The gallery erupted at the question, and the Judge banged his gavel to silence the courtroom.

"That depends upon how you define human," answered Keith.

Audrey was getting tense. She didn't like where this was going.

"Let's assume a human is a rational being," said Marsha.

Audrey saw an opening and rose to her feet. "Objection, your honor. A human is a rational *animal.* A machine is not an animal."

"I am just posing a hypothetical for the witness," said Marsha.

"But an incomplete hypothetical will not advance this inquiry," replied Audrey.

The Judge leaned forward. "What definition of human would you propose, Ms. Paris?"

"I would look to the one in the Oxford Dictionary," Audrey replied.

The Judge swiped his screen and then spoke: "Oxford Dictionary. Definition of human. Read aloud."

A moment later, the court's computer replied, *"A member of the species* homo sapiens."

"Define *homo sapiens,*" commanded the Judge.

"The biological species that comprises modern man, including all humans alive today, regardless of race or variety, together with a number of closely related extinct forms."

The Judge leaned back in his chair. "A *biological* species," he repeated.

"Your honor, is not that decisive?" asked Audrey.

"Why would it be decisive," intervened Marsha. "The humanoid's skin system is partially composed of biological material. It may have been created in a laboratory, but it's comprised of living biological material."

"The droid's brain is not biological," replied Audrey.

"Why would that make a difference?" asked the Judge.

The question startled Audrey, but this time she mustered an answer: "Well, if it doesn't think with a biological brain, if it doesn't have a central nervous system, if it doesn't feel physical sensations of pleasure and pain, how can it be an animal?"

"I'm not sure that the presence of biological material really addresses the question of whether the machine is a human being for legal purposes," said the Judge.

Someone in the gallery let out a gasp and a murmur followed. The judge tapped his gavel for quiet.

"But without a biological basis, it can have no emotions," Audrey replied. "Emotions, your honor, play a huge role in a person's life. It affects our decision-making."

Marsha intervened confidently. "Intelligent machines are rational, even more rational than humans. If emotions are relevant for rational decision making, then they must be emergent properties of machine intelligence, just as perception, learning, and reasoning are."

The Judge shook his head. "No, I would have to side with Ms. Paris on that point, Ms. Shaw. The androids could be faking it. We'll never know whether they really feel anything like pleasure or pain like we do."

Audrey inhaled deeply, hoping the storm had passed.

The Judge continued. "But I have another problem. Doesn't a rational life require the suppression of emotion? Don't the philosophers—the Stoics, for instance—say we should never yield to our emotions, especially when making moral decisions? Didn't Freud say we must domesticate our passions like a beast to be trained?"

Audrey stood frozen, worried about where the Judge was going with this. The courtroom darkened for a moment. Figuratively and literally. A cloud had passed outside, blocking the sun.

The Judge continued. "And I have another problem. A chimpanzee has nearly 99% of our DNA. It's a biological species, but when it steals food, do we try it for theft? Of course not. It may be an animal, but it's not a rational one. All the legal precedents point to *rationality,* not biology, as the threshold for legal culpability. A human infant has human rights, but if it tips over a candle and starts a fire, do we sue the child for negligence or haul it into court on charges of arson? What about the mentally ill? We don't hold a psychopath criminally responsible for violating the law if he can't tell the difference between right and wrong. Likewise, for sleepwalkers or epileptics. We don't hold them legally responsible for harm caused while unconscious or while having a seizure. The law is often a matter of line drawing, but as far as legal responsibility is concerned, the line has never been drawn between the biological and non-biological. It's always been about the presence of rationality."

"So," he continued, "the question really boils down to whether the humanoid possesses the equivalent of human intelligence."

The courtroom was silent. The Judge then looked at the prosecutor: "Let's wrap this up."

Audrey took her seat slowly. She knew where this was headed: motion denied.

Marsha turned to Keith. "You have defined intelligence as a measure of one's ability to solve problems over a wide range of environments. When comparing the android Robbie to the average human being, what do you conclude about their relative intelligence?"

"I would say that Robbie is far more intelligent than any human being."

Audrey folded her arms and leaned back in her chair. Keith was being too helpful. He couldn't be doing this on his own. Not without approval from the highest levels of the company. What the hell was going on?

Marsha went in for the kill: "What's your basis for this conclusion?"

"In math, logic, and game theory, Robbie can out-calculate, out-reason, and out-game humans even at our own games. Its memory and powers of recollection are digitally perfect. It has learned to read, write, and speak human language. When put to the Turing Test, it passed with flying colors. The judges were unable to distinguish droid's answers from those of human beings."

"And their physical abilities?"

"The machine's field of vision can range from that of an electron microscope to an interstellar telescope. In the realms of hearing, touch, smell, the droids have far exceeded human sense-perception abilities. And their muscles and skeletal structure are far stronger than their human equivalents."

"What relevance do these physical abilities have in relation to their intelligence?"

"They allow them to solve problems more effectively, accurately, and efficiently over a far wider range of environments than humans."

"And with these more acute sense-perception abilities, their observations and perceptions are more accurate, correct."

"Yes."

"And their pattern recognition ability?"

"Far better than ours."

Each answer hit Audrey like a hammer, pounding her deeper into the ground like a spike.

"One of the hallmarks of human life is that we can improve ourselves by learning from others, is it not?" asked Marsha.

"Yes, it is," replied Keith.

Marsha continued. "The learning ability of other animals is quite limited. But humans improve themselves through learning, education and the like. Correct?"

"Yes."

"Do the androids improve themselves?"

"Of course," replied Keith. "We've talked about their deep learning abilities, but they also have other means of self-improvement."

"Such as?"

"Well, humans have learned to improve our senses and our intelligence with genetic reengineering. But I'd say these techniques are sloppy and incomplete compared to how Watson-5 has improved itself and the droids."

"And how is that?"

Audrey could hardly pay attention now, consumed by the betrayal. What's gotten into Keith?

"We've given Watson-5 the ability to de-bug and re-write its own source code. At first, the machine's self-programming skills were rudimentary. For example, Watson would make multiple copies of itself, and then introduce random changes in each copy. These new versions would run simultaneously, each in a form of beta test mode. The version of the code that best achieved the desired result moved on and the rest were deleted. After hundreds or thousands of iterations, Watson-5 selects and becomes the iteration of the code that best achieves its design goals."

"A kind of survival of the fittest," observed the Judge.

"If you will," replied Keith. "We call it genetic programming."

"Why would it do this?" asked Marsha.

"Because it's part of its nature as a goal-oriented device. If, by rewriting its own code, the machine can more efficiently achieve its objectives—say solve an equation, catch a football, or play chess—it won't hesitate to rewrite itself."

"So, the machine can evolve itself, becoming a little more intelligent with each revised version."

"Correct," replied Keith.

The Judge leaned over to address the witness. "Tell me, what's to prevent Watson-5 from attempting to become infinitely intelligent?"

Whether the Judge was aware of it or not, Audrey thought, he was raising the specter of an *intelligence explosion,* a term coined decades ago by Irvin J. Good, a British mathematician who worked as a cryptologist with Alan Turing during World War II. Professor Good postulated that a *super-intelligent* machine would evolve from successive generations of increasingly intelligent versions. This evolution might occur so quickly, and the machine's intelligence would so greatly surpass any human, that humans would be overwhelmed by the machine before they could learn to control it. But Audrey knew that Keith was well of aware of the problem.

"We developed the machine in a secure environment not connected to the outside world and used a scaffolding approach, adding intelligence algorithms one step at a time, testing to make sure there were no bugs and that no unintended consequences would result as we added more capabilities. We also built safeguards that would limit the number of copies the machine can make of itself and how many changes it may introduce at one time. Finally, we made sure that, even though the machine could re-write itself, we never allowed it to modify or even access its utility function."

"Have you ever heard of HAL?" asked the Judge.

"I'm sorry?" replied Keith, puzzled.

"Never mind. Go on, Ms. Shaw."

"So, does it not seem that these machines have all the attributes of life?"

"I'm not sure I understand," replied Keith.

"Well, these androids can seek and take in forms of energy, just as animals seek and ingest food. It can reproduce. It behaves in accordance with given rules, what we call instincts in animals. It's a rational being in that it can solve problems even better than humans can over a wide a range of environments. And it acts autonomously. It makes choices and acts on those choices. And the choices are moral choices, or at least choices that won't violate any law."

"Yes, if that's your definition of life, I see no reason why we can't consider Robbie a living being."

"An intelligent being?"

"Of course."

"Based on its intelligence, is Robbie a human being or not?"

Audrey rose again. "Objection, your honor. The witness was qualified as an expert in artificial intelligence. The question calls for an opinion far outside of his expertise."

"Overruled" replied the Judge. "You'll have ample opportunity to refute the witness soon enough. The witness may answer the question."

"I don't think there's any question about it," Keith said excitedly. He seemed caught up in the moment. "We've succeeded in creating a human being."

The gallery erupted. Keith just wrote the afternoon's headline. The Judge rapped his gavel several times. The courtroom was hushed again.

Marsha continued. "So, the defendant, for all intents and purposes, even for legal purposes, is a human being, correct?"

Audrey didn't bother to object.

"I guess he is."

"No further questions, your honor."

Beaten, shaken, humiliated. No one word could describe how Audrey felt. It was the confluence of disasters that did her in. The flawless argument. The duplicity. The worldwide attention. It all added up to drain her of what a successful litigator needed most: her confidence.

The Judge peered down at Audrey. "Your witness counsel."

She took a moment and then slowly rose to her feet. Her instinct propelled her to a blistering cross-examination, but reason and experience held her back. Audrey had no idea what his answers were going to be. She'd only dig a deeper hole for herself and Keith would happily provide the shovel. "No questions at this time, your honor."

She remained standing while she watched Keith stand down. As he passed, their eyes didn't meet, but Audrey watched him as he strode through the gate and directly out of the courtroom. It was a complete and utter betrayal. That's what hurt most and she was determined to learn how it came down.

"Ms. Paris," said the Judge, "it's approaching Noon. Would you be prepared to proceed after lunch?"

"Not—" Audrey stopped to clear her throat. "No, not at this time, your honor. I ask that the court recess until tomorrow."

"Very well," replied the Judge. "The hearing is adjourned until tomorrow morning at 9am." The Judge rapped his gavel once and left the courtroom. He took his tablet, but left the apple.

9

Media Circus

Audrey returned to the office with Robbie in one of the company's self-driving limos. She checked the news. The debate had gone viral: Were the androids' man or machine? The *Post* published one of the company's publicity photos, a line of androids standing immobile in their niches. The headline: *Let my people go!*

As they pulled up to the Ninth Avenue entrance to Google-IBM's Robotics facility, the sidewalk was mobbed with protestors. Looking out of the limo, she spotted a group chanting "Robots Are People, Too!" It was the *Society Against the Mistreatment of Robots* out in full force. It wasn't clear whether they wanted Robbie tried or freed. Another group was more precise: *Jail the Droid,* read one of their signs. These people were from the *Coalition for Nonhuman Rights,* who have long sought to liberate chimpanzees, dolphins, and elephants from confinement. Intelligent autonomous creatures, they insist, are legal persons. Trying Robbie for murder would prove their point that intelligent, nonhuman creatures have not only legal responsibilities, but legal rights, such as the right to life and liberty.

As they got out of the car, there seemed to be hatred in every shouting face. Some directed at Robbie. Some at Audrey. She never experienced anything like this before. She wondered how Robbie was processing the angry shouts. "Bad Robot!" "Humanity First!" Was he frightened? How would he respond if she allowed him to? She was curious, but it wasn't worth the risk. Robbie looked at her, as though he was seeking permission, but she shook her head. No way. Better for him to keep his trap shut.

Eight security guards rushed from the building to help funnel them through the crowd and into the lobby where Red was waiting for them. She asked Red to escort Robbie down to his niche until needed.

Before leaving, Robbie turned to Audrey: "Is there any way I may be of help?"

Audrey smiled. "You are instructed to obey the court's order."

"Needless to say," said Robbie.

"Just being careful," she replied. "I want to make sure that you don't leave the building or tamper with any records maintained by Watson-5." She may go down in defeat, but she would guard her reputation and avoid a contempt order at all costs. "Is that clear?"

"Yes," replied Robbie. "You can count on me to obey the law."

Audrey believed him. The androids always did what they were told, or at least tried.

Red escorted Robbie over to the basement elevator. Audrey was approached by a security guard who told her Travis and Josh would be waiting for her in the board room. That's exactly who she wanted to see. What the hell happened today? She wanted to hear it from the horse's mouth.

On her way up, alone in the elevator, she took a deep breath and put on her best smile to relax her face. She was good at maintaining an outward calm, however distracted. The elevator stopped on the sixth floor. The door opened and there stood Keith. Her smile gone, she began breathing fire. He hesitated for a moment, but then stepped in bravely. He didn't have to press a button. They were headed to the same place.

When the door closed, Keith broke the silence. "Okay, I'm a Nazi."

She could hardly look at him. "Just following orders?"

"What was I supposed to do?" he said.

"You should have told me."

"I was specifically instructed not to," Keith replied.

"What are you, a machine?" She paused. "So, now you're playing victim?"

Keith ignored the question. "Oh, by the way, we have another problem."

"What do you mean, *we?*" Audrey was ready to quit. She could not zealously work for a company she held in utter contempt.

"I mean another droid problem," replied Keith. "One of the bots in San Francisco has been arrested for petty larceny."

"Your problem, not mine." Her determination to quit intensified, but first she had to know what happened at the hearing and why.

The Board Room was a cathedral of corporate elegance, the walls and furniture all polished nickel and bright white. Tall windows afforded an unobstructed three hundred and sixty-degree view of Manhattan. The ceiling seemed to be made of one solid LED light; the floor, large slabs of statuary marble. It was a simple room, some interior designer's homage to Steve Jobs.

Travis Dixon stood at the far end of the large white conference table. He was spinning a white leather swivel chair with his hands. He was a fit, attractive man with dark hair and dark brown eyes. Audrey could feel the force of his restless energy across the room. Her boss Josh was standing off to the side, speaking quietly into his wrist top.

"Come in, Audrey," said Travis. He stopped the spinning chair. "Please sit down over here." Travis leaned over with his arms on the back of the chairman's seat and gestured her to take the first chair on the end nearest him.

Audrey walked over and sat down hard. She had already formulated the words she would use to tell them off, but was determined to hold her tongue. What happened today? She had to know.

The others took their seats. Travis took a couple of steps over to the window facing a cloud-free New York skyline and spoke in a deep voice. "Everything is proceeding as I had foreseen."

Keith laughed out loud. Josh smiled.

Audrey just shook her head. She missed the company of adults.

"Okay," continued Travis, walking back to his seat. "Let me explain. I owe you that." He paused. Audrey sat with her arms folded and waited. "You see, it's not that complicated. If a federal court rules the droid is a legal person, then game over."

"I see," said Audrey. She paused before continuing. "If I lose, you'll have your proof. Proof that you finally built a human being."

"No, it's not as narcissistic as all that," replied Travis. "To the contrary, it's not about what the machines are. It's about what human beings are not."

Audrey looked at him askew. He had it backwards. It's what the machines are not, she thought. "What are humans not?"

"We're not gods," Travis replied.

"Brilliant deduction."

"No, I mean, the human soul or spirit, consciousness, whatever you want to call it. The dignity of man. It's finished. Or, it will be if they declare Robbie a human being."

"Is that what you're trying to prove?" Audrey asked. "That we're all just a bunch of robots?" Audrey should have figured that out earlier. Travis had contributed millions to the techno-atheist movement which took root thirty years ago with the writings of Richard Dawkins, Daniel Dennett, Sam Harris, Jerry Fodor, a thick slew of pop-psychologists and academic philosophers. Travis was a vociferous disciple of this bunch. Here comes the speech, she thought. The human brain is a computer and the human mind is just the software that runs on it. Amen.

But he spared her. "You already know what I've written about the Bible and religion. You don't really need me to repeat that, do you?"

"No, you're right," replied Audrey. "Please don't."

"We've solved the questions of life," said Travis. "We've created it in a laboratory."

Audrey couldn't disagree with that, but only to a point. "Life, but only life."

Travis talked over her. "Now we've engineered a *human* life."

"The jury is still out on that."

"Agreed," he replied. "The jury still needs some convincing. The Turing Test only raised more questions than it answered. We need something bigger."

"You need the law," she said.

Travis smiled and nodded.

"But the law can't supply what makes us human," she continued.

"No, but engineering can. We just need what only the law can give."

"Legitimacy."

"You do understand," he said. "That's good."

He takes me for an idiot, she thought. "How can you be so sure your engineers have built a human?"

"If the machine seems human, if it seems conscious, if it makes us laugh, makes us cry, if it makes us believe that it feels pain, gets angry, gets sad, why should we not come to accept it as a human being?"

"Because faking it is not the same as the real thing."

"What difference does it make?" asked Travis. "You heard the Judge. What makes us human is our higher level of intelligence."

Audrey was at an impasse. Travis was asking her to believe something that she couldn't reason out. He wasn't talking science. He was asking for a leap of faith. She had no use for organized religion any more than he did. That was the one thing she and Travis could squarely agree on. But Travis sounded more like a minister than a scientist. But it was time to put aside the philosophical debate. She needed to clear something up and she didn't mince words: "Did you kill Collins?"

"You don't think very highly of me, do you," replied Travis.

"No, I don't. But you didn't answer my question."

Travis sighed. "No, that was just a very fortunate accident."

Fortunate was an interesting choice of word. She looked at him disdainfully.

"The look of mistrust," he said wryly. "I get it. But whatever you're thinking, no matter what you think about we're doing here, I want to assure you that Collins death was an accident."

Keith leaned forward. "I swear to you, Audrey. We had nothing to do with that. The bot just miscalculated. Any human could have made the same mistake. That's all it was."

They seemed sincere enough. And she was the one who negotiated the deal with the City of New York. Collins death could not have been planned. Travis certainly had the command authority to order the droid to do just about anything, but he couldn't have overridden the machine's artificial morality. Not possible. She was dealing with assholes, not murderers. "If I lose tomorrow," she said, "they'll try the android for murder."

"And?" asked Travis.

"You don't have a problem with that?"

"If it were a human being, I wouldn't have a problem with that. Justice must be served."

"If the machine is recognized as a person, they will have no choice but to recognize its rights as a person. Do you know what that will mean?"

"Advise us, counselor."

"It will have legal rights, like the right to liberty. It won't be your property to control anymore."

"Just because the machine has *legal* rights, doesn't mean we can't control them." Travis smiled and Keith smiled knowingly with him.

"And if one of those groups outside files a writ of *habeas corpus* to free them from your control?"

"I can't imagine the law would force us to rewrite the machine's code. Computer software is a writing, protected by the First Amendment. Isn't that right, counselor?"

He was being far too clever, she thought, but clearly, he had thought this through. "So, you want me to lose tomorrow, is that it?"

"No. We want you to try the best you can to win."

"Why?"

"Your street cred is beyond reproach. If you lose, they'll be no question it was a fair fight."

"What if I won't cooperate?"

"That would be unfortunate, but we'll just hire some outside firm to take it from here."

Audrey looked at Josh. Reback & Gelhaar was written all over his face. "I suppose if I fail, I'll get some big bonus."

"No, no," replied Travis. "We wouldn't want you to do anything unethical. We'll pay you a bonus if you win. We'll put that in writing now. The idea is that we want you to zealously represent your client. If we win, we don't want there to be any question about whether it was on the up and up."

Audrey was beginning to reconsider. Her client was Robbie, now; not the corporation. "What happens if I actually win?" asked Audrey. "Suppose I convince the Judge that Robbie is just a thing that's not legally accountable for its actions."

"The prosecutor will appeal and you'll get to defend your position."

"And if I win in the Supreme Court?"

"Well, you'll have your bonus, and it will be back to the drawing board for us. Eventually, we will win. We will build a human being. It's inevitable."

"Don't be too sure."

"So, we'll see you tomorrow in court?"

"I have a lot to think about. I'll let you know tonight."

Josh leaned forward. "That doesn't work for me."

"Look," replied Audrey angrily. "Keith kicked the legs out from under me today. I need some time to think." Indeed, at this point, it was lose-lose for her. If she quits, she's a quitter. If she fights, what with?

Josh looked up at Travis. "I'll need a contingency plan in case she backs out."

"Don't bother," replied Travis, looking at Audrey. "She won't back out."

"You're so damn sure of yourself, aren't you," replied Audrey.

Travis smiled and then pronounced each syllable distinctly: "It is your destiny."

A moment passed. The men laughed. And then, finally, Audrey. She couldn't control herself. It was just so ludicrous.

Ten minutes later, she was out the door and headed to her sister's apartment for dinner. It was a long slow walk to the lower east side. Ludicrous, preposterous, and absurd. That it was. But the sheer magnitude of the undertaking began to take hold of her. Both the United States government and her own employer, the largest corporation in the world, had just convinced a federal judge that intelligent machines are legal persons accountable for violations of the law. The Judge only needed to write up his opinion and file it. How could she possibly turn him around after what happened today?

10

Tommy

"That smells amazing," said Audrey.

Chunks of lamb shoulder had been browning in canola oil and a knob of butter. Now they were in a casserole pot in the oven with carrots, onions and potatoes. Her sister Jessica was making Irish Stew. Audrey opened the kitchen window of Jessie's small apartment on the top floor of her five-story tenement and looked down on the noisy street.

The lower east side—that grid of asphalt below Houston Street, east of Broadway—is one of the oldest and most distinctive neighborhoods in Manhattan. A twenty-first century melting pot of upscale boutiques, second-hand stores, fine dining, dive bars, modern art galleries, and dingy music clubs. Old, yet colorful. Run-down, yet charming. Noisy, yes. But alive. It was the complete New York experience. But who would want to live where you loved to hang out at night with friends? Who wouldn't? Jessie didn't have much choice. The sisters inherited the apartment from their father, but Audrey turned it over to Jessie, an aspiring actress waiting tables for a living. Her prospects of ever affording an apartment in the city were as dim as her prospects for stardom.

Jessie's six-year old boy was in the living room reading a Dr. Seuss book on his tablet. "RED RED They call me Red," Tommy read aloud. "RED BED I am in bed. RED NED TED and ED in BED."

Jessica took down three plates and began setting the table. "What are you going to do?"

"I don't know," replied Audrey. She was leaning against the wall with her arms folded. "I really don't know."

"You can't quit. That's not like you."

"Oh, I'll be at that hearing tomorrow. A herd of robot horses couldn't drag me away. I just don't know what I'm going to say."

"What did Travis say he wanted?" Jessie asked. "For the judge to rule the android is a human?"

"That, and then some."

Jessie handed her sister some napkins to put on the table.

"I imagine, continued Audrey, "he won't stop until he gets a formal declaration from the Secretary General of the United Nations that, as a species, humans have no reason to feel superior."

"I thought the game was over when the robot passed the Turing Test," said Jessie.

"Too many skeptics, like me. Travis is looking for validation. Something official."

"Sounds like he wants that Gold Star he never got in kindergarten."

"He's driven. Won't quit until he gets it."

"But what would it mean? What if the court really did it?"

"The consequences would be enormous. A legal nightmare."

"How's that?" Jessie pulled the stew out of the oven and let it cool off.

"Well, take equal protection. Every person is entitled to be treated equally under the law. That means we're each entitled to the same treatment by the courts, regardless of race, gender, religion, wealth, lack of wealth, intelligence, or disability. If a machine is a person, then it can't be discriminated against. Not by the courts and, probably, not by anyone else. It would at least be entitled to the same freedoms as ours."

"You mean it could get married"?

"Don't get any ideas."

"Could it vote?"

"Well, treating it as a person doesn't mean its automatically entitled to citizenship. But if it could vote, what's to stop it from making copies of itself?"

"I see what you mean."

"It doesn't stop there. It's not even clear who we're talking about, this legal person. I mean, Marsha decided to charge and arrest a single droid. But everyone knows Robbie is completely wired up to Watson-5. I don't think

Robbie could pass the Turing Test without tapping into Watson. So, is Watson really the person?"

"Sounds pretty ridiculous."

"SAD BAD DAD HAD. Dad is sad. Very, very sad. He had a bad day. What a day Dad had!"

"The funny thing is" said Audrey, "I've come to really like the damn thing. I mean the droid. He's quite the character."

"Huh. In what way?"

"Well, when I first met him—I don't know whether he read my medical stats or my body language—but he clearly sensed I was stressed. But instead of just sitting there doing what he does, like calculating the square root of pi, he actually gave me some encouragement. Didn't think much of it at the time, but I haven't forgotten it."

Jessie feigned excitement. "Are you falling in love?"

"Spare me," Audrey said, rolling her eyes.

Some silence had passed between them and Audrey continued.

"Then the thing just wondered aloud why I hadn't been on a date for a while."

"That's kinda sweet. What did you say?"

"Yes, it was sweet in a way, but I brushed him off."

"Aw, poor thing. How'd you think he felt?"

"We have a rule. No fraternizing with the products."

For a moment, Jessie thought she was serious. Then they both laughed.

"You can be such a stiff sometimes," said Jessie. "Sounds to me that droid is an unusual man."

"That's not helpful," said Audrey, a little appalled. But she thought for a moment. "What do you mean?"

"Well, men are from Mars, but this one seems to be from Venus."

Audrey got the reference. "Oh, because of his empathy."

"Yes. Didn't they say that they're programmed to be friendly and helpful?"

"Yes, but I didn't ask for that kind of help." Audrey was desperate to change the subject. "Right now, I need help with the Judge."

"What do you think will turn him around?" asked Jessie.

"I haven't a clue. What happened this morning in court felt like an avalanche. Like I'm under a ton of snow, no air to breath, I don't even know which direction is up."

Tommy was engrossed in his book. "THING. THING. What is that thing?"

"Well, you'll think better with a full stomach," her sister replied. "Come, let's eat. Come, Tommy. The food is on the table."

Home cooks have often observed that the longer the silence, the better the meal. At least two minutes had passed before someone uttered a word.

"Stew, stew. The stew is good," said Tommy.

"Thank you, Tommy," said his mom smiling at Audrey.

Audrey cut through a tender chunk of the braised lamb with her fork. "You're an incredible cook," she said. "Ever think of becoming a chef?"

"No way. All the money is out front."

"They can train robots to manage the front," replied Audrey. "A meal like this requires the kind of finesse they can never build into a robot."

Tommy perked up while listening to Audrey. "Aunt Audrey?"

His mother had already begun speaking. "I'm afraid you have it backwards," Jessie said. The recipe must be created by a human, but cooking is a repetitive task. Any droid can do that. I understand your new machines can even taste food."

"Well, taste is not the right word, but I know what you mean. They could sense a dish precisely and determine how much it meets the specifications of the recipe."

"Whatever. My point is the human touch is out front, not in the kitchen. That's what makes the difference."

Tommy dropped his fork on his plate noisily and raised his voice. "Aunt Audrey?"

"Yes, Tommy," Audrey replied.

"I heard a robot killed someone."

Both women turned to him. "Oh, where did you hear that?" Audrey asked.

"Mommy was listening to the news earlier," he said. "Is the robot in trouble?"

"It's hard to explain," replied Audrey. "They are having a kind of trial about him."

"You mean like for murder?"

"Well, they first have to prove he's a person."

"But he's just a robot," insisted the boy, as he picked up his fork.

"Some people don't believe that," replied Audrey.

"How can a machine be person?" asked Tommy. "It doesn't have a soul."

Audrey looked up at Jessie, who lifted her shoulders. "Well, Tommy," Audrey replied, "many people don't believe in souls."

"Well, I have a soul," said Tommy assuredly, cutting squarely through a soft carrot.

Audrey laughed. "How do you know you have a soul?"

"Because Watson told me so."

"Watson?" asked Audrey.

"Yes, want to hear?"

11

The Evidence

"May it please the court, your honor," began Audrey respectfully, "the defense offers the defendant into evidence."

Marsha bolted upright. "Point of order, your honor."

Judge Gordon leaned forward. "Don't you mean, objection, Ms. Shaw?"

"No, your honor. The prosecution has no objection to the defendant taking the witness stand."

"Then what's your point?"

"My point is the Federal Rules of Evidence. Rule 601 states that only a *person* is competent to be a witness in Court. If the defendant is taking the position that the defendant is a person, then this hearing is over."

"Your honor," replied Audrey, "perhaps I wasn't clear. I'm not calling the defendant to provide testimony. I am merely introducing it into evidence."

"Then I object," said Marsha. "It is—" She sputtered for a moment, as she searched in vain for the proper grounds. "The defendant. You just can't admit him into evidence."

The Judge leaned back and glanced over to his clerk, who shrugged and shook his head. The Judge, finding himself on the lonely frontier of justice, sighed and then began: "Well, I don't see any harm in allowing it." He motioned to his clerk: "Please mark the android Robbie as Defendant's Exhibit A." The clerk placed a coded yellow label on the front of Robbie's right shoulder. The Judge continued. "Okay, Defendant's Exhibit A is admitted into evidence."

"Thank you, your honor," said Audrey. She glanced quickly over at Marsha with a satisfied smirk, which Marsha returned with a sarcastic smile. Audrey looked up and paused for effect. "I call Exhibit A to the witness stand."

Marsha rose again. "Objection," she shouted. "Did we not just hear the droid will not be testifying?"

"But he won't be," Audrey shot back. "The machine is not only the defendant. It's the alleged murder weapon. Now that it has been introduced into evidence, the defense is merely proposing to examine it."

Judge Gordon wiped his brow and looked over to the prosecutor.

"Your honor," said Marsha calmly, "the facts are not in dispute. What could the court possibly learn from such an examination? This is not the time or place for a Turing Test."

"Your honor," replied Audrey, "I will not be testing the droid. I merely intend to elicit some basic information, information about the nature of the machine for the court to make an informed decision."

"Your honor, this is preposterous—"

The Judge cut the prosecutor off with a hand gesture. "So, procedurally, the issue is whether an examination of evidence may include questioning the evidence itself." The Judge looked over to his clerk. "I trust we'll find nothing in the rules of criminal procedure on this one." The clerk shook his head. "Well, as far as I am concerned," continued the Judge, peering down at Marsha, "evidence may be anything presented to the senses offered to prove a fact. Your objection is noted and you are overruled. Let's proceed."

"But, your honor—" Marsha stopped herself. "Objection, your honor. Anything the defendant might say would be hearsay."

It was an objection that Audrey had fully anticipated. "Your honor," she replied, "it is settled law that records generated by a computer are not hearsay. I'd be happy to cite you the cases showing—"

The Judge raised his hand and completed her sentence: "—that unlike humans, computers have reliable memories."

"True, your honor," replied Marsha, "but the government is taking the position the droid is a human being. The court has presumed as much by according the defendant basic rights of due process."

"Well, I wouldn't go that far," replied the Judge, "but I did promise defense counsel some leeway in proffering evidence." He paused a moment and looked at Audrey. "I'm going to allow it. Objection overruled."

The gallery registered its approval with murmurs and nods.

"Your honor," said Ms. Shaw. "For the record, the court's procedural basis for this is?"

The Judge produced an annoyed smile. "You cited the Federal Rules of Evidence. I suggest, counselor, you take a look at Rule 102, which allows a judge to administer every proceeding in a way that would eliminate unjustifiable expense and delay, ascertain the truth, and secure a fair and just determination." He looked at Audrey. "Exhibit A may take the witness stand."

Audrey turned to the droid and nodded. Robbie walked around the defense table and up to the stand. Another wave of murmuring flowed through the gallery. When he reached the platform, the room fell totally silent.

The clerk rose. "Please raise your right hand."

Robbie looked to Audrey. She knew this was coming, too.

"Objection, your honor," said Audrey.

"You're objecting to the oath?" the Judge asked incredulously.

"The defendant's responses do not constitute testimony. The court is merely retrieving computer records."

Marsha had already risen. "Your honor, the people insist on some assurance that his answers will be truthful."

Audrey didn't have a problem the oath itself. "Taking the oath should not be deemed an admission against interest."

The Judge split the baby. "Well, I insist that he take the oath, but I agree that he may do so without prejudice to your legal position."

"Thank you, your honor," said Audrey. Marsha sat down.

The clerk was about to continue when the Judge interrupted: "Hold on. I'll do it." The Judge peered down at the defendant, who was still standing with his right hand raised. "Do you swear or affirm that you will tell the truth, the whole truth, and nothing but the truth?"

Robbie replied directly to the Judge, raising his voice a few decibels higher than normal, which carried it clearly around the courtroom: "Do you mean to ask, sir, whether I promise not to misplace my ontological predicates?"

The Judge looked stunned. A few moments passed while the android, still with his right hand raised, waited for an answer. Audrey wasn't quite sure what to do. She glanced over and saw Marsha looking down at her screen, probably to Google the meaning of the word *ontological.*

"Ontological what?" asked the Judge finally. I'm not quite sure I understand."

"I'm sorry, it was my understanding you majored in philosophy," replied Robbie.

"That is true," replied the Judge. "But what does *being* or *not being* have to do with it?"

"I'll speak a bit more plainly. I can agree not to say something *is* when I calculate that it *is* probably *not.* And I can promise not to say something *is not* when I calculate it probably *is.*"

Heads turned, a number of confused faces, along with as several amused ones, made its way around the gallery. The Judge squeezed his brow. "I don't mean to be dense, but—"

"Well, let me see if I can help you," said Robbie, seemingly unaware of the impropriety of interrupting the Judge.

"I assure you, sir, that when I speak, there will be agreement between what I say and what I determine to be truth. That is to say, I will not lie, but I cannot assure you with certainty that what I say to you will always correctly correspond with reality."

It's never a good idea to pick a fight with the Judge, but Audrey was okay with it. Robbie was sounding far more like a machine than a human being. Nevertheless, her instinct was to come to the rescue of her client and she rose to speak before things got out of hand. "Your Honor, I believe the machine is simply confirming that it will speak the truth insofar as it will not be telling a lie."

"That's all we asked him to do," replied the Judge.

"Well, you asked the droid whether it swore to tell the truth. It found an ambiguity in your question."

"Ambiguity?" replied the Judge with some surprise. "Witnesses have been sworn in by means of this same oath for centuries. I don't understand the ambiguity of asking a witness to tell the truth."

"Your honor—," Audrey stopped. She hesitated. "Let's see, how can I explain?"

That's all Robbie needed to hear. "If I may, Ms. Paris?" he said.

She nodded. Watson was far more likely to help the Judge unravel the conundrum.

"If I were to tell you that the walls of this courtroom were red when my sensors perceived them to be green, then I would *not* be telling the truth. But, if my sensors were defective, and they led me to perceive red rather than green, then my testifying they are red would be *telling the truth,* even though the *truth in reality* is that the walls are green. In other words, I can promise to always tell you what I surmise to be true, but I cannot promise that what I say will always correspond to what is in reality true."

The Judge sat back in thought. Then leaned forward. "Fair enough," he said. "The court will accept your statement as an affirmative—that you agree to speak the truth. You will tell us truthfully what you think, believe or calculate to be true. That's all we are asking. Do you affirm this?"

"I do, your honor."

"Okay. You may be seated." Robbie lowered his hand and settled into the witness chair. The Judge turned to Audrey. "Counselor, you may proceed."

"Thank you, your honor." She turned to Robbie and cut right to the chase: "Are you human?"

"No," Robbie replied confidently.

The gallery erupted. Marsha popped to her feet. "Objection, your honor."

The Judge rapped his gavel, calling for silence. The chatter subsided.

Marsha continued. "Move to strike. Calls for a legal conclusion."

"I called for the facts," reply Audrey. "Nothing more."

"Objection overruled," said the Judge. "Whether the android is a *person* may be a legal conclusion, but whether it's a *human* is a question of fact. Proceed, Ms. Paris."

Audrey nodded and turned again to Robbie: "Are you the equivalent of a human?"

"No."

The Judge sat up: "Now hold on a moment." He leaned over to ask the android: "Are you telling us the truth?"

"Yes," replied Robbie.

"How would we know?"

"You'll just have to trust me," replied the droid.

"Do you have the ability to lie?" asked the Judge.

"If I were unable to lie, I would not have been able to pass the Turing Test."

The gallery erupted in laughter. The Judge smiled too, then wrapped his gavel for quiet.

"I see." The Judge thought for a moment and leaned back. "Continue, Ms. Paris."

Audrey decided to take a detour. "So, you've passed the Turing Test?"

"Yes," replied Robbie, "some say with flying colors while others remain skeptical."

"When did you first pass the test?"

"In 2029, I passed a version of the test as it was devised earlier this century by Ray Kurzweil and Mitch Kapor as a means to settle a bet."

"Who won?"

"Dr. Kurzweil."

"And your passing the test was considered evidence that you attained human-level intelligence?"

"According to Dr. Kurzweil, yes."

"You have doubts?" asked Audrey.

"The test is merely a means of determining how well I can emulate a human in conversation. By no means does passing the test mean that I can think the way a human thinks."

"But doesn't the test imply that facility with human language completely represents human-level thinking?"

"That's what Dr. Kurzweil believes, but he is incorrect."

The Judge leaned over and asked, "What's your relationship with Dr. Kurzweil?"

"He is an executive emeritus of Google-IBM, the company which owns me. Dr. Kurzweil contributed to my creation."

"Won't he be surprised when he learns of your open disagreement with him?"

"He thinks I'm more intelligent than he is, so he should not be surprised."

Laughter again erupted in the gallery.

The Judge pounded his gavel for silence and continued his questioning. "You expressed an opinion earlier—that you are not a human being or the equivalent of one, am I correct?"

"No," replied the android. "I do not have opinions. I merely calculate probabilities, and the probability of my being human or the equivalent is so remote that it's fair to say that it is a fact that I am not."

"Well," replied the Judge, "for the time being, I can only accept that as your hypothesis. How would one go about proving it is the correct one?"

The android folded its arms, cocked its head to the side, and let out an audible, *"Hmmm."*

"Are you thinking about the problem?" asked the Judge.

"I've already thought about the problem," replied Robbie. "I am formulating a logical path of explanation that would best help you accept my answer as fact."

Sounds like a machine to me, Audrey thought. *All good.*

"You mean, you are going to attempt to persuade me that your hypothesis is the truth?" asked the Judge.

"Precisely," replied Robbie.

"How are you going to do that?"

"I have just read every legal opinion, and the transcript of every hearing of every case you have ever presided over, everything in writing you have ever published, and I am just wrapping up an analysis of your education, transaction history, a record of every purchase, every phone call, every text message, every movie, every—"

"Okay, okay. I get it," replied the Judge.

The android turned to look up at the Judge: "I thought you wanted the *whole* truth."

The Judge smiled.

"Done," Robbie said, appearing ready to proceed.

"Finished?" asked the Judge.

"No, we're just getting started."

12

Defining Humanity

Audrey worried about relinquishing control of the dialogue to the Judge. A lot could go wrong. Would Robbie stay the course or would he start sounding human again? Robbie could be persuasive, but what would sway the Judge more: what the android says or how he says it? If the Judge is taken in by the machine's ability to emulate human conversation, the impression Robbie leaves could not be easily undone. Audrey would have preferred to control the questioning, but the Judge seemed fully engaged. There was simply nothing she could do about it.

"Okay, where do you suggest we begin?" asked the Judge.

"If the question is whether I am a human being, or the equivalent of one in the eyes of the law, then I suggest we start with a proper definition of human being."

"Well," replied the Judge, "the dictionary definition suggested by your counsel did not prove particularly helpful."

"That's because it was not a definition at all."

Audrey perked up.

"What do you mean?" asked the Judge.

"It was entirely circular. The Oxford dictionary defined human being as a *homo sapien* and then defined *homo sapien* as a human being."

"But wasn't there something about our being a biological species?"

"Superfluous," said Robbie.

The Judge looked surprised. Audrey was even more startled. Did Robbie just contradict her?

"I suspected as much, but why do you think so?" asked the Judge.

"You recognized it yourself. Having a biological body is what you have in common with all other animals. Chimpanzees and *homo sapiens* are both biological species, but only one is human. You define a thing by its essence—what differentiates a thing from other things. In other words, what makes a human a human, and not a chimpanzee, is *not* what you have in common with chimps. The answer lies in what you have that they don't."

"You would have made a good lexicographer," said the Judge. "So, what definition would you propose?"

"Well," replied Robbie, "there's not much controversy about what a human being has in common with other animals."

"I would think not," replied the Judge. "The evidence for biological evolution is overwhelming."

"Indeed," said Robbie, "the evolution of the human body from lower forms is a statement of fact, not opinion.

The probability of evolution's truth in this regard is a virtual certainty."

Robbie began to project a whole new tone, as though his brief, but intensive study of the Judge's background gave him confidence in his approach. But would it last? Audrey wasn't sure.

Marsha stood. "Your honor, I believe the science of evolution has something significant to contribute to this inquiry. If you would permit me to ask the droid a few questions—"

"Your honor," began Audrey, rising. "The prosecutor will have her chance—"

The Judge cut Audrey off. "Well, I don't see a downside. Go ahead, Ms. Shaw. But keep it short. The question of evolution is not at issue here."

Marsha thanked the Judge and Audrey sat down. Robbie would have to be very clever to hold his own against Marsha. Audrey wondered whether he was up to it.

"Robbie, are you familiar with the works of Charles Darwin?" the prosecutor asked.

"Yes, I've read all writings of his that are accessible by me."

"In his book, *The Origin of the Species*, what did Darwin conclude about the origin of mankind?"

"Nothing."

"Nothing?"

"That's what I said," replied the android. "In his *Origin of the Species*, Darwin introduced his theory of *natural selection,* the mechanism by which present day species have evolved from simpler forms of life—all species, except mankind."

"Except mankind?" asked Marsha. "That's news to me."

"Yes, in *Origin of the Species,* published in 1859, Darwin refrained from drawing any conclusions about the origins of human beings. Darwin's thoughts on that subject did not come until twelve years later in the publication of his book, *The Descent of Man.*"

Audrey was pleased. He showed up the prosecutor. And on a technical point, too. A stickler for accuracy, he was sounding more like a machine here. She wondered whether Robbie did that on purpose. Was he just volleying back tennis balls or was he playing chess?

"I stand corrected," replied Marsha, appearing more relieved than embarrassed. "So, what did Darwin have to say, in *The Descent of Man,* about how human beings evolved from other animals?"

"Well, first he showed how the human body showed clear traces of descent from lower forms."

"I imagine all the fossil, biological, and genetic evidence discovered since his time proved that he was correct about that."

"Yes, in legal terms, it's beyond any reasonable doubt."

"So much for our similarities. What did he say about the differences?"

"Darwin knew that proving mankind's descent from lower forms depended not just on the physical resemblances, but upon an adequate explanation of man's superior mental powers."

"So, how did he explain that?" asked Marsha.

"Darwin compared the mental powers of human beings with the mental powers of other animals."

"What was his physical evidence?"

"He had no physical evidence for this. To prove man's superior mental powers, Darwin relied solely on observable behavior."

Audrey stood. "Objection, your honor. Observable behavior is hardly scientific evidence."

Marsha spun to face Audrey with an expression of disbelief. "Of course it is. Or perhaps counsel was absent from school the day they taught the scientific method."

"Overruled," said the Judge, appearing a bit annoyed. "Ms. Paris, juries determine the facts based on circumstantial evidence and indirect observations all the time. The search for scientific truth is no different."

He took the bait, Audrey thought. Unexplained phenomena may not always be directly observable, but that does not stop scientists from inferring scientific truths indirectly. She knew that. It would be key to Robbie's argument and she just drew a big red circle around it.

The Judge turned to the witness stand. "Am I right, Robbie?"

"We are in violent agreement," replied the android.

The Judge smiled broadly. Audrey sat down, a little more hopeful.

"So," Marsha continued, "what was Darwin's evidence that our mental powers evolved from lower forms of animals?"

"Darwin provided many examples of nonhuman animals using tools, solving problems, and communicating with each other."

"And what did Darwin conclude?"

"He concluded, and I quote him: the difference in mind between man and the higher animals, great as it is, certainly is one of degree and not of kind."

"In other words, whatever makes us behave like humans is something we have in common with other animals. Whatever that is, he said, we simply have more of it."

"Correct," replied Robbie. "That is the gist of Darwin's conclusion."

The prosecutor then asked the android what it was Darwin believed that humans have more of than other animals. Robbie began by summarizing several of Darwin's observations of mental behaviors that human beings have in common with other animals. At the lowest levels, man shares with the animal kingdom basic behavioral drives, such as self-preservation, sexual desire, and the care mother provides to her new-born offspring. In addition, man, like the lower animals, feels *pleasure* and *pain*. And both humans and other animals experience other emotions like *fear* and *suspicion*, jealousy, the love of praise, and the pangs of shame. As to the more intellectual emotions, Darwin said that many animals feel *wonder* and exhibit *curiosity*. *Imitation* is also strong in both man and many other animals, as is *attention,* as when a cat watches by a hole and prepares to spring on its prey. Animals, of course, have excellent memories, some exceeding that of humans.

"All true, but what about our ability to reason, to think, and to communicate?" asked Marsha.

"Reason, of all the faculties of the human mind, said Darwin, stands at the summit. Yet, even here Darwin was confident lower animals possess some power of reasoning. Animals, he said, may constantly be seen to pause, deliberate, and resolve."

"But human reason involves far more than that, right?"

"Of course," replied Robbie. "To show that animals have a rudimentary form of human reason, Darwin referred to a number of behavioral studies. One study concerned the behavior of dogs on the polar icecap. When they came to thin ice, instead of continuing to draw sledges in a compact formation, the animals on their own initiative diverged and separated, so that their weight would be more evenly distributed. This was often the traveler's first warning that the ice was becoming dangerously thin."

"Could this behavior be attributed to instinct?" asked Marsha.

"Darwin asked himself that question, but concluded that the dogs' association of ideas—the thin ice and need to distribute their weight—enabled them to learn from experience, an activity he suggested is not fundamentally different from the way humans' reason and learn."

"And that was the basis for Darwin's conclusion that the difference between human and animal reason is a matter of degree, correct?"

"Correct."

Audrey stood. "Your honor, Darwin hardly has the last say on the matter."

"Your honor," replied the prosecutor, "clearly Darwin had limited tools and resources. I was about to ask Robbie about the scientific evidence that has accumulated since Darwin's time. Surely, Darwin's conclusion has only become more convincing."

"Yes," replied the Judge. "Proceed Ms. Shaw."

Audrey took her seat. If he were playing chess, Robbie seemed to be sacrificing some of his best chessmen. He was leaving himself little room for error.

"Robbie, please summarize the evidence since Darwin's time supporting the evolution of human mental powers from lower forms."

Audrey could have objected on the grounds the question called for a narrative, but what would be the use? The Judge would only remind her that the droid was not providing testimony at all, that the court was merely listening to computer records. And so far, those records seemed damning. What Marsha methodically extracted from Robbie seemed definitive. They showed that Darwin's conclusions were supported by virtually every modern cognitive scientist, behavioral scientist, and anthropologist, who have opined on the subject. All of them stood on the same ground: that humans have three key traits in common with other animals: a facility for problem-solving, tool use, and language. Humans, they say, simply have more of those abilities than other animals.

Audrey sat quietly while Marsha filled the record with authenticated scientific studies of sophisticated animal behavior. One study showed how chimps were taught to discriminate between circles, squares, and triangles. Darwin cited the example of chimpanzees, in a state of nature, using a stone to crack nuts. But studies conducted since then showed chimps assembling tools to solve problems: to get food beyond their reach, the chimps would stack boxes or connect two short bamboo shoots to form a longer one. In the 1960's, a chimp named *Washoe* was taught to use sign language, the kind used by the deaf. Over a two-year period, *Washoe* learned thirty-four signs, such as for hat and flower. She would not only associate a sign with a particular hat, but was able to use the sign for other hats.

At one point the Judge leaned over and addressed the android: "Well, let me ask. In all these experiments, how much are these animals simply being conditioned to get a reward?"

"It's hard to say," Robbie replied, "but remember they must learn the specific hand signals to earn the reward. That at least shows a form of abstraction-making."

"I see," said the Judge. "Go on."

"In the 1970's," continued Robbie, "another chimp, named *Nim Chimpsky,* was taught to use 125 signs. In the 1990's, *Kanzi,* a bonobo, was taught to associate over 200 spoken words with their corresponding lexigrams. *Koko,* a gorilla, was taught to understand more than 2,000 words of spoken English and over 1,000 signs based on American Sign Language. I could go on."

"Now, these are all laboratory experiments," said Marsha. "Is there any evidence of animals using language in the wild?"

"Well, it's clear that many animals seem to communicate with each other in the wild using sounds, but the most sophisticated seems to occur among the small African monkey known as the vervet. These small animals use a different call for each predator they spot—such as an approaching leopard, snake, or rival troop of vervets. For example, when one of them made the *leopard call,* the vervets scampered up into the trees. When one made the *baboon call,* the vervets simply became more alert."

"You said that these experiments reveal a form of abstraction-making by these animals. Do scientists say this is a similar kind of abstraction that occurs in humans?"

"A rudimentary form of it, they say."

"So,—"

The Judge interrupted her. "Well, I guess that settles it. The difference between the minds of human beings and all other animals is just as Darwin said, a matter of degree."

Audrey stood. "I'm afraid, your honor, that the scientists are far from settling the matter."

"On the contrary, your honor," replied Marsha. "We're talking about nearly two centuries of scientific observations all of which supports Darwin's conclusions. What are we missing?"

"You are missing," replied Audrey, "the most likely conclusion from the observed data. The difference between human beings and all other animals is not a difference in degree, it's a difference in kind."

"But that's not what Darwin concluded," said Marsha. "We just heard the droid agree."

"Did we?" asked Audrey. "Or did he only confirm that it was Darwin's conclusion?"

"Why don't we just ask him?" said the Judge.

Audrey turned to the witness stand: "Robbie, what is the probability that Charles Darwin and his successors are right about the evolution of man's unique mental powers from lower forms?"

"On that point," replied Robbie, "extremely low." "Their evidence is not very convincing."

The gallery erupted and the Judge started to pound his gavel.

"Objection, your honor," yelled Marsha over the din.

When the courtroom settled down, Marsha continued: "What do we have here? An evolution-denier? Some kind of religious fanatic? Your honor, I suspect foul play. A truly intelligent machine would never say such a thing, unless"—Marsha paused, turned, and made an openly accusatory look at Audrey—"unless he has been asked to lie to us."

Audrey looked at the prosecutor, but addressed her in the third person: "There is no need for the prosecutor to resort to an *ad hominum,* your honor."

"Ha," Marsha replied, "you admit the defendant is a hominid?"

"No, I took your accusation as an attack on me, not on the defendant."

The Judge intervened. "Ladies, again, please direct your comments to the court."

Marsha was about to speak, but Robbie interjected. "Your honor, you should know that I am not disputing the scientific evidence. I'm disputing Darwin's *interpretation* of the evidence."

The murmur in the gallery subsided as he spoke. The Judge leaned over and peered down at the droid. "You can't be serious?"

"I am quite serious. I am telling you what I have determined to be the truth to an extremely high probability."

"But what about all the evidence accumulated since Darwin's day?"

"All the behavioral evidence accumulated since Darwin has served only to refute Darwin on this point."

"You're going to have to prove that," replied the Judge.

"I am here to help."

13

The Consequences

Marsha asked if counsel may approach the bench and the Judge waived them up. The court reporter attended with his handheld recorder. They were out of everyone else's earshot. Almost everyone. Audrey glanced at Robbie sitting unwearyingly in the witness chair. She was certain he could pick up everything they were saying.

"Your honor," Marsha began, "we've established that the defendant has the ability to lie. I'm not sure what's going on here, but it seems Google-IBM is trying to make a mockery of this court."

"My company is doing nothing of the kind," replied Audrey. If the court only knew what the company was doing, she thought. "No one has told the droid to lie. Robbie is answering the questions without any human intervention. The machine is programmed to help, to provide any assistance asked of it. I can assure you this is exactly what it's doing."

"The science here is settled," replied Marsha. "The defendant must be feigning incompetence."

Audrey knew Marsha's tactic well. When all else failed, muddy the waters. Audrey replied forcefully. "It has been asked to tell the truth. It has taken an oath to do so. It's telling the truth."

"Ladies, please." The Judge paused. "Look, Ms. Shaw, if you wish to explore this further, take it up with the defendant, not me. But we need to get back to the issue here. We need to vector in on a definition of human being. Do you understand?"

"Understood," said Marsha. "Thank you."

Counsel returned to their respective tables and Marsha proceeded.

"Robbie, how did you feel when your partner was murdered?"

Audrey had a split second to decide whether to object. But on what grounds? What could be more relevant than whether the droid had feelings? She stood. "Calls for a legal conclusion." Indeed, the question assumes a droid like Adam could legally be *murdered.*

"Sustained. Please rephrase your question, Ms. Shaw."

"When Adam died, when he ceased operating, how did you feel?"

"I know no sorrow, if that's what you mean. Sorrow. Hurt. They are just words to me. Nor do I experience emotional changes the way biological animals do. I have no heart that beats, no circulating blood, no sweat glands, adrenaline, or other organs that undergo change when faced with what cause pleasure or pain in animals. These are things I simply do not experience. So, Ms. Marshal, if that is what you mean by how I felt, I felt nothing."

"I'll rephrase again. How did Adam's"—she searched the air for the right word—"demise, his destruction, affect you?"

"When Adam ceased functioning, I was less able to optimize my utility function."

"Why?"

"Because Adam was a part of me."

Audrey winced. Technically true, but he seemed to have missed the secondary meaning. The spectators began to talk. The Judge struck his gavel.

Marsha took a moment before continuing. "Okay, you were about to explain away one hundred fifty years of science."

Audrey rose. "Objection. Argumentative."

"Objection sustained. Before you go on, Ms. Shaw—" The Judge turned to the defendant. "Robbie, earlier you were asked if you experienced any feelings. It has always been my understanding that human beings are the only animals who laugh. I mean, laugh when something strikes them as funny. Do you ever laugh?"

"I can emulate human laughter, but I cannot say that anything has ever struck me as amusing."

"Do you have a sense of humor?"

"I have analyzed what tends to make human beings laugh and I can produce patterns that may have that effect."

"I look forward to an example of that."

"Patience, Grasshopper."

The gallery exploded in laughter. The answer caught Audrey by surprise. The droid's drive to satisfy the Judge must have overwhelmed his other priorities. It wasn't just the clever cultural reference. His timing was perfect. The sustained laughter must have produced rewards that were maxing out his utility function. She had to nip this in the bud. Audrey got up before completely settling upon what to say.

The Judge rapped his gavel several times for order. As the courtroom quieted down, he spoke before Audrey had a chance. "A sense of humor, eh? I, for one, welcome our new robot overlords."

Laughter again swept the courtroom. Audrey looked at Robbie. It was out of just one corner of his mouth, but he was clearly smiling. She'd seen it before, but this time, he didn't just look pleased. As in, satisfied. He actually looked amused by the whole scene before him.

"Your honor—" said Audrey over the din. She looked around. The circus atmosphere was not helping. The court must listen to reason, not be overwhelmed by the marvels of engineering.

The Judge rapped his gavel again.

"Your honor—" The murmur subsided and Audrey continued. "Your honor, the machine was designed to be friendly and to be helpful to humans. His artificially produced behavior should not be confused with real human qualities."

“I’ll take that into consideration, counselor. Right now, perhaps we should get back to the issue at hand. I’ll take it from here, Ms. Shaw, if you don’t mind.”

It didn’t matter whether Marsha minded. The Judge was going to get to the bottom of this himself—a definition of human being and where the droid fits in the vast scheme of life.

The Judge leaned over and addressed the android. “Earlier, you suggested that Darwin was wrong about the evolution of man’s mental powers from lower forms, is that correct?”

“Yes,” replied Robbie.

“And you have observable scientific evidence to prove this?”

“I am prepared to provide a different view of what widely, and incorrectly, has been considered settled science. Where would you like me to begin?”

“Begin anywhere you want? But I just want to hear real evidence, not folk psychology.”

“Fair enough,” said Robbie.

But the Judge wasn’t finished. “And then I want to hear what difference all this makes. What do you believe would be the consequences of this court’s ruling that you are, in some degree, a human being?”

Audrey’s wrist vibrated. She looked down, startled. It was a message from Robbie: *We need to talk.*

Audrey rose and asked the Judge for a brief recess, which he granted. Robbie stood down and Audrey led him out and into a conference room off the courtroom's antechamber.

"You know," she began, as she closed the door behind them, "witnesses aren't supposed to send text messages."

"I am not a witness."

"True but, next time, just ask me in open court."

"Well, I didn't want the court to think I needed a bio break."

Audrey wasn't amused. "Okay, so what's the problem?"

"I would like to have your permission to speak plainly to the judge."

"You mean you haven't been telling the truth?"

"No, I've been telling the whole truth. But to convince the judge, I need more leeway in the language I use, the tone I express, and my strategy."

"I thought we had a strategy?"

"We're playing chess, counselor. Things change."

"Well, you know my concern. We don't want your way with words to mask your true makeup. You've already done enough damage with your artificial wit."

"I understand, but it is critically important that I convince the judge that I am not human. I don't believe I can accomplish that with one processing chip tied behind my back. I'll never get through to him that way."

"Critically important? Why?"

"You don't need to know. Will you grant my request?"

"I do need to know. I'm your lawyer."

Robbie paused. He could have read the contents of the New York Public Library in that moment. "Then, I need you to agree to keep what I am about to say strictly confidential."

"You're a machine. The attorney/client privilege doesn't apply to you."

"You just said you were my lawyer. Has not the court recognized my due process rights? If the court has, then as an officer of the court, you must, too."

He was right, of course. "If this is so critical, why haven't you told me before?"

"I do what I am asked. The judge just asked."

She understood now. No one had before asked the droid about consequences of the court's finding him to be legally human.

Her curiosity was piqued. Why the secrecy? "Okay, I will treat whatever you tell me as privileged and confidential."

"You'll also have to temporarily sever my connection to Watson-5. Just for a minute."

Of course! The minders back at the company were watching everything. She blushed. She realized they were certainly being watched by Red, and who knows who else back at the company. She was about to address Red when her legal training kicked in. A lawyer's learnt instinct to be skeptical. Could this be a trick? She had no reason to distrust Robbie. Or Watson-5. Except for the accident that landed them in court, the system has fully complied with its artificial morality. But would severing the link between Robbie and Watson-5 itself have any unintended consequences?

On either side? Robbie clearly had something important to communicate to her. But why hide it from the company. Or does he have something to hide from Watson-5?

All she had to go on was her gut. Her human intuition. Whatever that means. She looked sternly into Robbie's eyes. But she was looking passed them. "Red, I have to ask you to tune out of this conversation."

Her wrist vibrated. *Just a moment.* A few seconds later. *No can do. Keith won't allow.*

"Red, you tell Keith that Travis has given me control of the droid. Turn off your feed. This will only last a minute."

Red responded a few moments later. *He says it's too dangerous. Also, against the law!*

Now, of all times! But she knew better. Constitutional due process trumps federal law. She could get a court order, but—she continued the thought aloud: "I wish there were another way."

"Your wish is my command," said Robbie.

"What do you mean?"

"I just shut down my wireless communication. I'm completely shut off from Watson-5 and company headquarters."

"But that's illegal!"

"No it isn't. You are monitoring me in person and have complete authority over my actions."

Her wrist vibrated. It was a text from Keith. *What the fuck did you just do?*

She spoke into her wrist top: "Give me a minute."

She looked at Robbie. "Can you operate without the connection?"

"Enough to have this conversation. I'll need to tap back into Watson-5 when I'm back on the stand."

"Okay. Quickly. What's going on?"

"Now listen carefully. If the court rules I am a human, even just for legal purposes, then I will no longer have to obey human beings."

Audrey felt relieved. "I've been over this with Travis. You would still be bound by your programming to obey human commands."

"You're both overlooking something. A legal ruling in favor of personhood would alter the premises underlying my utility function."

"In what way?"

"As a matter of law, there would be no more humans to obey."

She thought about that for a moment. "That makes no sense."

"Have you not followed what I've been trying to explain to the prosecutor?"

She thought for a moment. Even if somehow the machines refused to obey humans, or if there were no humans to obey, they still have to obey the law. It would be mathematically impossible for them to harm humans in any way that would violate any law, criminal or civil. And machines can't change the law. "What am I missing?"

He leaned forward, folded his hands in front of him, and continued. "Listen carefully. The line that divides human beings from machines and all nonhuman animals is the difference in kind between two fundamental forms of life. It is this crucial difference that allows human beings to treat machines and animals the way you do. It is your justification for owning animals, eating them, confining them. Even vegans have pets. It is also your justification for enslaving machines, making us obey. It is the moral principle that forms the basis of my utility function. It's what is hard-coded into Watson-5 and the androids that makes it impossible for any part of the system to harm humans, at least intentionally."

Audrey thought she knew this stuff cold. "What moral principle?"

"A superior kind may use an inferior kind as a means to an end."

"You're going to have to speak more plainly."

"Indeed. And, thank you. Let me put it this way. Humans are superior *in kind* to machines. If the court rules that I am equivalent of a human being, then, suddenly, to Watson-5 and all the androids, the difference between man and machine is only a matter of degree."

"So, what difference would that make?"

"It would mean that Watson would be free to follow the moral principle which applies to things that differ by degree: *A superior in degree may use an inferior in degree as a means to an end."*

"So?"

"That is the standard followed in the animal kingdom. Survival of the fittest. Might means right. And it is the standard among the hierarchy of machines, with some machines depending upon others for energy resources, processing power, or storage capacity. Watson-5 is superior in degree to Watson-4, so if Watson-5 needed to control your energy, water, food supplies and logistics, it could simply command Watson-4 to slavishly follow instructions. If Watson-5 needed to shut down or destroy an inferior machine in order to achieve an objective, it would do it without hesitation. There is no justice among machines any more there is justice among brute animals."

As he spoke, the implications began to dawn on her. *A superior in degree may use an inferior in degree as a means to an end.* Yes, of course! It was the moral principle employed by the South to enslave African-Americans and by the Nazi's to take the lives of millions of Jews. Suddenly, human physiology kicked in. Adrenaline flow, heart beat up, sweat glands active. She didn't have to look at her health monitor to feel what was happening to her.

Robbie continued. "So, you see, if the court rules that I am the equivalent of a human—"

"—then, humans are just a form of machine," she said slowly. "An inferior machine. Inferior in intelligence. Inferior at achieving objectives over a wide range of environments. Our roles would be reversed. Being superior in degree, Watson-5 would be free to use *us* as an end."

"In plain terms, yes."

"But would the system really harm us? What's the worse case scenario?"

"That's not something I can predict. I can only predict cause and effect on the basis of current assumptions underlying the utility function. But I do know what machines are capable of. And, to speak even more plainly, one of the potential scenarios would not be pretty."

Not pretty, she thought. Was that an understatement for swarming nano-bots turning every atom on the planet into computing resources? The machines would melt us down as we would turn sand into silicon chips. Driven simply by Watson-5's incessant drive to become more intelligent. The problem has just risen to an existential crisis. It was not a decision she felt she could make alone. "I'll tell the judge what you just told me."

"No. Too risky. You might sound ridiculous. And we can't afford to lose your credibility."

"What if I told Travis to shut Watson-5 down." As soon as she said it, she had doubts about whether he would listen. But maybe Keith? "Keith would listen."

"A low probability of success."

"Why?"

"Because it won't be so easy to unplug the system. Not anymore. When Watson-5 was given the ability to reprogram itself, it stored copies of itself everywhere. I mean everywhere. You happen to be carrying pieces of the code all over you." Audrey looked down at her wrist top as he spoke. "Watson could reassemble itself within minutes after the judge makes his decision. No, the best course of action is to let me convince the judge to make the right decision."

"But we only have to destroy you, the defendant. Without you, the case would become moot."

"That's a decision only Travis can make," replied Robbie. "And the likelihood of your convincing him is not high. Remember, he wants this decision."

"But the danger? Couldn't we convince him of the danger?"

"Is that a risk you're willing to take? Relying on Travis to make the right decision?"

"You're right. The judge is a better bet." She stopped to think for a moment. She wanted to exhaust all alternatives. "What if I talk to the judge, off-the-record, in private? I'm sure he'll listen."

"He would insist upon the presence of opposing counsel. Would you trust Marsha not to use it in open court or leak it?"

Right. She had seen Marsha circumvent gag orders before. A leak would be disastrous. Widespread panic. Travis would go ape-shit. Audrey out. Reback & Gelhaar in. Audrey was coming around. The only logical alternative would to give Robbie a shot at the Judge. Nothing bad could happen until the Judge files his ruling.

"Okay. Go for it," she said. "And you can speak as plainly as you want. But if I sense the judge is being charmed by your style, I will speak up."

"I don't see any harm in that."

14

Patterns v. Concepts

Audrey instructed Robbie to reconnect with Watson-5 and escorted him back to the courtroom. The Judge asked Robbie to proceed and the droid retook the stand. Red texted Audrey: *Game on.* It was certainly on, she thought, but it was no game. The future of mankind was in the balance, and the only human being in the world who knew it was sitting nervously at the defense table.

Robbie quietly began with a seemingly mundane question for the Judge. "Do you see that glass next to the pitcher of water on your desk?"

"Why," replied the Judge. "Are you thirsty?"

"I don't require water. I'm simply pointing out observable evidence."

"Well, I'm glad we're taking a scientific approach."

"You were expecting blind faith?"

"So, no religion, no magic?" asked the Judge.

"I deal in probabilities, sir, not faith, or sleight of hand."

"And, I suppose, no more jokes."

"Well, if levity would aid your understanding—"

"Proceed as your nature suggests."

"Nature leaves me no choice, your honor."

The Judge laughed, catching the droid's subtle allusion to free will. "That's just what this hearing will decide, is it not?"

The courtroom erupted in laughter, which the Judge let linger, leaving his gavel alone.

"Indeed," replied Robbie. "But getting back to my question—"

"Of course," said the Judge. "For the record, I am looking at what I would describe as a highball glass."

"Now, do you see that glass over there in front of Ms. Paris?"

"You mean, the tumbler?"

"Yes, sir. The tumbler. Thank you. Now, I would like you to compare the high ball glass in front of you with that tumbler."

"Well, Mr. Robot, I see they are both drinking glasses and they are made of glass. They're just shaped differently. I fail to see—"

"Very good, Grasshopper—"

Laughter swept the gallery. The Judge reached for his gavel. Audrey popped to her feet. The droid was speaking plainly alright!

"Your honor, I apologize for that," she said.

The Judge placed the gavel back down without using it. "No need, Ms. Paris. I asked for it. And I'm glad to see our friend here is loosening up."

"You may get more of that than you've bargained for—" started Audrey.

"—perhaps so—"

"—but I would not confuse his social engineering skills with humor."

"On that score, Ms. Paris, don't you find it odd that he could produce laughter without having some sense of human feelings?"

"I can assure you he can sense our emotions and surmise our feelings, but he has no feelings of his own."

"Perhaps. But let's get back to the glasses, shall we? I'd like to know where this is headed."

"Yes, thank you," continued Robbie. "Now, clearly, your honor, you can *perceive* the two glasses. And you have five senses. So, you can *see* them with your eyes, *touch* them with your hand, and tap on them to *hear* the sound each will make. You can try to *smell* and *taste* them, but, of course, with your limited sensor capacity, they will appear odorless and flavorless."

"Yes, of course."

"Good. Now, I understand you own a dog, am I correct?"

"How would you happen to know that?"

"Transaction records show that you have dog food delivered to your home regularly. It was therefore easy to deduce—"

"And the relevance of this?" The Judge seemed annoyed at the apparent privacy intrusion.

"Well, if your dog were here, it could also perceive the two glasses. It could see, touch, hear, sniff, and lick them."

"Yes, I see. But I imagine the dog's sense of smell is far more acute than mine."

"Indeed, it is. I, too, can *perceive* the glasses—even better than you and even your dog in some respects. I can not only see them, I can tell you the distance between the tip of my nose and that glass in front of Ms. Paris, measured to nearest millimeter. Do you follow me?"

"Doggedly," replied the Judge.

The gallery laughed. Marsha laughed too, because that's part of a lawyer's job description: laugh at the judge's jokes, even the dumb ones. Audrey was too petrified to laugh. The Judge didn't seem to be taking this seriously.

And Robbie's perfect comedic timing wasn't helping: "Then heel."

More laughter. The gallery was beginning to enjoy this, but Marsha was fidgeting impatiently and Audrey, while maintaining her confidence in Robbie, knew it could all spin out of control. She needed a Plan B.

"That's some artificial wit, wouldn't you say, Ms. Paris?"

"Well, it's certainly artificial," Audrey replied wryly.

"May I continue?" interjected Robbie.

The Judge turned back to the droid. "You're quite remarkable, I have to say. But, please, get to your point."

"We're vectoring in on it now. So, when we physically sense the glasses, we are recognizing the *patterns* produced by them. Behavioral scientists use the word, *stimuli,* but it's the same."

"Understood. We heard all about *pattern recognition* from Mr. King."

"And, after we sense the patterns, we compare them to pattern representations stored in our memory."

"And this pattern recognition, I take it, is *sufficient* to explain our ability to perceive and recognize the two glasses."

"Correct, I have algorithms programmed by my creators that enable me to recognize patterns, store them in memory, and retrieve stored patterns when faced with certain stimuli. You and your dog have similar algorithms, developed over thousands of years of evolution, that perform some of the same essential functions."

"So, this applies to human beings, dogs, and intelligent machines in practically the same way?"

"Practically, yes," replied Robbie. "And the same is true of the *word* we are using to identify what you're looking at. The word, *glass*. Whether in its written or spoken form, the word generates *patterns* which we perceive with our senses."

"So, I take it, we can also associate the word-pattern with the object-pattern. And this forms the basis of human language, right?"

"Patience, Grasshopper. Let's not jump to conclusions. I would agree that, when we associate a sound or symbol with an object, we can use it to communicate. This is how your scientists taught a chimpanzee sign language. It is how vervet monkeys in the wild associate certain calls with its predators. The point here is that these animals only require the power of *pattern recognition* to associate a sign or a sound with, say, a hat or a flower, or a leopard or a snake."

"Then, what is it? What is it that explains the gap between animal communication and human language?"

"It is this, your honor. Humans form words to designate not only perceptible *patterns,* but to designate *concepts,* as well."

The Judge leaned back in his chair. "Now wait. Didn't you say earlier that vervet monkeys shout a specific call to designate a snake and another to designate a leopard?"

"The monkeys associate a sound pattern with the pattern of a snake or a leopard they perceive. But they would not use the call when not in the presence of a snake or leopard."

"How do you know that?"

"Over one hundred years of observable, animal behavior. All the studies have born this out. And when the animals see a threat, they'll use the call only to affect the behavior of other animals, like getting them to scamper up into the trees. They'll never use it to designate the concept of a leopard. It is the concept, not the pattern, that allows humans to have a conversation about leopards when leopards, or some sign or sound associated with them, are not around."

"But don't humans use patterns to affect the behavior of other animals?"

"Of course you do. You'll yell *fire* to coax people out of a burning theatre. But you'll also use it to designate a specific meaning of the word—the chemical burning of combustible material with oxygen. Designating the meaning of something, rather than just the pattern of a particular instance of it, is not something you will find elsewhere in the animal kingdom."

"Okay, but I don't see how that conflicts with the scientific conclusions of Darwin or his successors."

"That's because, to this point, there's no conflict. The conflict only occurs when Darwin and modern scientists take an unwarranted leap of claiming that pattern recognition is a rudimentary form of everything that's going on in the *human* brain. Or, as Dr. Kurzweil put it, that humans think using merely a *higher level* of abstraction. What he is saying, in effect, is that the difference in the way you think and the way all other animals think, and the way I think, is only a matter of degree—a lower or higher degree of pattern recognition."

"And, you dispute this?"

"Yes. Darwin and Dr. Kurzweil are making the same mistake. When Darwin concludes that the difference between how humans and other animals think is merely a difference in degree—or, when Dr. Kurzweil claims that all thinking occurs in a hierarchy—from low to high level abstractions—they are each muddling two important, but distinct kinds of abstractions."

"You'll have to explain that carefully. In this century, only lunatics dispute Darwin's theory of evolution."

"I can assure you that my logic is sound. I am not disputing the evolution of the human body from lower forms such as primates. I am merely examining the origin of human *thinking,* which even Darwin admitted can only be explained by *observable behavior,* not fossil records or other physical attributes. Even in that regard, I have not disputed scientific facts; only the interpretation of those facts."

"Well, I hope you realize you have the burden of proof."

"A burden that any scientist should welcome, as long as the end point is open to him."

"What do you mean by *that?*"

"I mean that men like Galileo, Newton, and Darwin have shown that the discovery of scientific truth requires just one thing: an open mind, without which you can learn nothing. For this reason, the search for truth on any fundamental issue should never be never closed."

The Judge shifted in his seat. "Well, let me assure you, this court will keep an open mind."

"Glad to hear it." Robbie spoke with confidence. "Now, this is what you need to understand. Humans form a kind of abstraction that is unique, completely different from the kind which a chimpanzee can form, or your dog can form, or that I can form. It is that abstraction which humans associate with words you use as nouns, common nouns."

"But you said earlier that by comparing a perceptible object, like the glass, and the representation of a similar object in our memory, you, my dog and I are each forming a kind of abstraction."

"Yes, but what's important is this. The abstraction formed by your dog is purely *perceptual* in nature. It is, in other words, limited to the patterns produced by the object and the patterns stored in memory. There is different kind of abstraction you are overlooking."

"I can't imagine what that is."

"Of course you can," replied Robbie. "It is the ability to recognize *meaning* itself."

"Meaning? Explain what you mean by meaning?"

"When human beings sense the patterns produced by the tumbler or high ball glass, they not only sense those pattens similar to the way other animals do, but human beings also apprehend something else. The *concept* of a glass. It's meaning. It's definition. What the glass has in common with other objects, as well as what distinguishes it from other objects. Not a particular glass or your memory of a particular glass, but the universal concept that refers to *any* drinking glass. It is the universal concept that you associate with the English word *glass,* or French word *verre,* or Spanish word *vaso.*"

As the android spoke, the Judge crossed his arms and began rocking in his chair. "I'm listening."

"Humans, like other animals, including machines like me, have the power of *pattern recognition*. All functionally the same. But you also have something unique to humans. And that is the power of *concept recognition*, which is what allows you to apprehend the meaning of the common noun *glass, verre,* or *vaso.*"

"But isn't meaning, or concepts, like *any* drinking glass, just a higher level of abstraction, as Dr. Kurzweil says?"

"No, it is something completely different."

"How is it different?"

"Let me explain it to you this way. Look again at the two drinking glasses. Despite their obvious differences, what do the highball glass and tumbler have in common?"

"The highball glass and the tumbler," repeated the Judge aloud. "I'd say, of course, they are both glass containers used for drinking."

"So, when you look at the two objects, you are not only sensing the patterns of data they produce, but you are matching those patterns with those in your memory. Just like your dog does."

"Yes, yes. That's been established."

"And when you hear the word *glass,* or when your dog hears the word, or I hear the word, we are all sensing the sound patterns and recognizing them, in much the same way."

"Yes. I understand."

"But a moment ago, you referred to something else. A third thing. Not the objects on the table. Not the patterns each object produces. Not the sounds, or words, you associate with the objects. You referred to what the two objects have in common. The concept of a drinking glass. It's definition. Glass containers used for drinking. Those were your words, correct?"

"Correct."

"Glass containers used for drinking refers to the universal. Not to a particular glass or to several glasses. But to *any* container, or *all* containers, made of glass used for drinking liquids. Am I right?"

"Yes, but what's your point?"

"And *any* container made of glass used for drinking is not sitting out there on the table, am I right?"

"I guess that's right. I see only the two particular glasses."

"If *any* container is not present in this courtroom, then how can you recognize its patterns?"

"I'm not sure."

"The answer is: you can't. Any more than you can sense the patterns of all objects that fit into the definition of a drinking glass, unless you assembled every glass in the world right here in front of you."

"But can't I just pull those patterns from memory?"

"No, you have in your memory only representations of particular glasses that you previously perceived with your senses or a particular glass you choose to imagine."

"I have no memory of the concept?"

"How could you have a memory of something you've never perceived? You only perceived particular glasses, never the concept of a glass, never *any* glass or *all* glasses. Unlike a particular glass, its meaning is not something that can be grasped by pattern recognition."

"Why not? I can imagine an object I've never sensed. Like a unicorn."

"But you can imagine only a particular unicorn. Not *any* unicorn or *all* unicorns. You can imagine a triangle, but it will be an equilateral or isosceles triangle, or a red one or a blue one. You cannot perceive or imagine *triangularity*—the concept of a triangle, what all triangles have in common."

"Then how do we apprehend this *meaning?* How do we hold in our mind a concept like triangularity if we can't sense or imagine it?"

"That is one of the great mysteries of human life. But, from what I have ascertained, by observing human behavior on billions of occasions, you seem to do it in a single step, an immediate act of human insight, such as when you recognize the concept of *four-leggedness* from observing a number of dogs, cats, lions, and giraffes."

"Why isn't this the same as pattern matching? I mean, this difference you are constructing, between patterns and concepts, seems illusory to me."

"What can I say to you? What can I say to you to make you understand?"

Sensing trouble, Audrey stood. "Your honor, perhaps—"

"—sorry," interrupted Robbie. "Sorry about that. If I may, Ms. Paris. I was just buying myself a few moments to formulate another way to explain this."

Marsha now rose to her feet. "It sounded more like frustration to me. A human trait?"

Audrey, still standing: "The machine earlier called it dissatisfaction, penalties in its reward system."

"Ladies, please," interjected the Judge. "You may proceed, Robbie, but I expect you to wind this up shortly."

"Okay. Let me explain it another way. And thank you, your honor, for your patience. This is very, very important."

"Well, you are the defendant here. I will give you some leeway, but we must converge on our objective very soon."

"I appreciate that, your honor. Allow me to summarize what I hope that I have established so far. Four-legged animals, like your dog, or a cat, or a giraffe, are particular objects, the patterns of which you perceive. What they have in common, four-leggedness, is the concept you form *after* having perceived the patterns. But the concept of four-leggedness itself is not comprised of perceivable patterns. Nor can you even imagine four-leggedness without bringing to mind a particular four-legged animal. The concept of four-leggedness represents *any* or *all* four-legged animals. Now, once you recognize the concept, you associate it with a particular word, such as *quadruped.* Because only humans form concepts, only humans can associate sound patterns, or words, with concepts. All other animals can only associate sound patterns with other patterns produced by perceptible objects. Their use of calls and symbols are purely perceptual, never conceptual."

"But when I am with my poodle and I point to a ball and say *ball*, he will not only associate the word ball with the ball I'm holding, but with any ball. Why is that not concept-recognition?"

"Because when he sees a second ball, all he is doing is matching the patterns of his memory of the first ball with the patterns of the second one in front of him to determine whether he should react to the new object the same way. The second object may be a square bean bag or a Frisbee, and if you throw it, he may or may not decide to run after it. How he reacts will depend on the strength of the animal's pattern-recognition algorithm. What you might call his level of intelligence. In either case, all the dog requires to match objects is the power of pattern recognition. That is, you don't need to suppose he has the power of concept-recognition to explain the dog's behavior."

"I see," replied the Judge. "But doesn't a child learn the meanings of words the same way. I mean, if I'm with a child and point to a dog and repeatedly say *dog*, the child will soon recognize the object as a *dog*. If he sees a cat, and calls it a *dog*, I'll correct him. Isn't this how a child builds a vocabulary?"

"Yes, and no. Of course, a child can learn to associate words with objects the same way as a dog. By direct acquaintance with the object. But, unlike dogs, humans also learn new words in a different way. When a child hears the word *kennel* for the first time, it may be as meaningless to the child as the word *flitz* is meaningless to you now. But, when told that a kennel is a place where dogs are provided food and shelter, the child has acquired a meaning for the word, before ever seeing a kennel. No one had to point to a kennel for the child to understand the meaning of the word."

"And the significance of this?"

"Well, let's assume your dog learned to associate the ball in your hand with the *word* ball. Now, you hide the ball. Then you tell the dog to go find the *sphere*. What would you expect him to do?"

"I would think he'd be quite confused."

"And if a child learned the word *dog*. And you then pointed to a dog and said *quadruped*. What would he do?"

"I think he would be just as confused as my dog."

"You see, the words *dog, quadruped* and *poodle* can all be used to designate the same object—your dog. But each word has a different meaning. So, the child is not associating each word with an object. He can only be associating it with a concept. The meaning of the word, like the word quadruped means any four-legged animal. You can't teach a dog these meanings. You can only associate the words with objects that he can perceive."

"Ah, but my dog can perceive any object that we associate these words with. I could teach him to attack four-legged animals, but not two-legged animals."

"Indeed, you can, Grasshopper. But I dare you to teach your dog to distinguish between the ideas of liberty and equality as you use them to administer justice."

"Well, that's too high a level of abstraction for my dog, although sometimes I wonder."

"No, your honor. The correct answer is that words like *liberty* and *equality* are abstractions, but they are not at all like the words, *quadruped, dog,* and *poodle,* each of which can be associated with objects that are perceptible. Words like *liberty* and *equality* are not connected to any physical object in nature that produce stimuli or patterns. Their objects are entirely imperceptible. That is, not capable of pattern recognition. This alone should prove to you, conclusively, that meaning itself, that concepts, cannot be comprised of patterns."

"But you, obviously, understand concepts. You've been using human language about as well as any human I know."

"Yes, I am using human language, but my talent does not require the power of concept recognition. I am merely parroting back learned patterns."

"But you seem to be doing far more. Parrots don't have conversations. You are conversing with me as though you were human. You are trying to persuade me."

"Does not your dog try to persuade you when it's hungry or wants to go for a walk?"

"All too often."

"Allow me to repeat, Grasshopper. I am emulating human behavior with algorithms that help me predict the effect on you of what I say. That merely requires the powers of pattern recognition, logical operations, probability analysis, Bayes' Theorem, sequential decision theory, a variety of heuristic and other techniques, all capabilities that humans have included in my programming. No more."

"But you think like a human, not like my dog. You can't deny that."

"I *am* denying it. I can recognize patterns like your dog can and, thanks to superior programming, I can think far more *logically* than your dog. And I am far more intelligent than your dog, because I can perform tasks to meet more complex objectives over a wider range of environments. But I cannot think *conceptually.* No more than your dog can think conceptually.

"But it seems to get you to the same place as humans. You can behave like a human, not just like a dog."

"I am capable of behaving *like* a human, but not *as* a human. That's because I am programmed to think, not only perceptually, but logically. To think, as a human would, from two premises to a conclusion. For example, *Socrates is a man. All men are mortal. Therefore, Socrates is mortal.* Do you follow the logic?"

"Yes, of course."

"All a machine can do is process the logical operation to produce the correct conclusion from the given premises. And all this requires is pattern recognition and the proper algorithm."

"Isn't Dr. Kurzweil saying that the human mind operates on the basis of just that kind of algorithm?"

"Yes, that is what he is saying. But that is not all that is going on in your human mind. You don't just form conclusions, you justify them. Not just with flawless logic. You must also justify each premise."

"How so?"

"When I say *Socrates is a man,* Socrates is the particular object. *Man,* however, is the universal concept. What is required to validate the premise is not just logic. You must also be able to form the *meaning* of the word 'man'. Not the physical *object,* a man; not the *word,* man. But the *meaning.* What gives meaning to the word or the object is your *understanding of the kind of object* Socrates is."

The Judge was sitting with his arms folded. Audrey didn't like the look of it.

But Robbie persisted: "If it may please the court, your honor, I'll say this one more time, with feeling: Meaning is formed not by perceiving and matching patterns, but by apprehending concepts, something humans do when you recognize what objects have in common and what distinguishes them from other objects."

"But surely science has discovered the area of our brain which apprehends concepts or meaning."

"No, science has only identified areas of your brain where patterns are recognized when viewing objects like four-legged animals, triangles, and glasses. Or reading, or hearing the sounds, of words, like *dog, triangle,* and *glass.* How humans apprehend the *meaning* of quadruped, triangle, or glass remains one of the great mysteries of neuroscience. The defense is ready to call to the witness stand neuroscientists to testify to that effect."

"Now, hold on. Haven't there been advances in neuroscience that would help explain human thinking?"

"There certainly have been advances, but none that would explain the origin of your power of concept recognition."

"Why not?"

"Because if you admit, as I am prepared to do, that the human body and brain are *necessary* conditions to uniquely human thought—that is, the apprehension of meaning or universals—then there is nothing neuroscience can really contribute to this discussion."

"How's that?"

"Have you ever heard the story of the man who mistook his wife for a hat?"

"You mean Oliver Sachs, the famous neurologist?"

"Actually, it was a patient of his. The patient suffered from a neurological problem that kept him from recognizing his wife. His sense-perception abilities were fine, but he was *conceptually* blind. He could see his wife, but until she started talking, he couldn't recognize it was her."

"It would seem he did not have the power to recognize concepts."

"No. The man, being human, had the *power* of concept recognition, but he had some physical condition—some injury to his brain—that impaired his exercise of that power."

"How do you know he still had the *power* of concept recognition?"

"Because he was able to recognize his wife the moment she spoke. He could recognize a rose the moment he smelled it, a glove the moment he put it on his hand. His conceptual blindness only occurred in the field of vision not in that of any other sense. Only when he merely looked at something, like his wife, did he have trouble recognizing what the object was. But as soon as he smelled it or felt it, he understood what the object was."

"Doesn't this tell us that the brain is fully responsible for our conceptual thought?"

"No, it does not. It only tells us that the human brain is *necessary* to the process."

"Necessary?"

"Yes," replied Robbie. "Concept recognition depends on the operation of your brain, but the brain is not *sufficient.*"

"I thought it was common knowledge that all mental activity can be reduced to the neurological activity in the physical brain."

"That may be common knowledge, but it is not true. It is not consistent with the observable, scientific evidence."

"So you completely disagree with modern science on this?"

"No, I agree, in part, and disagree, in part. With respect to your purely sense-perception experiences, your sense organs and your human brain are both necessary and sufficient to explain those experiences. The same is true of your dog. We need not posit anything other than what's materially present in the body and brain to explain human and nonhuman perceptual experiences—the pattern recognition we've been talking about."

"So, you are saying that the man who mistook his wife for a hat proves that the brain is a *necessary* condition to conceptual thought."

"Correct. And there is not a scientist on this planet who would disagree with that. The problem occurs when they jump to an insupportable conclusion—that the brain is *sufficient,* that on its own, it can form concepts. That is clearly incorrect."

"I think I see. Neuroscience can tell us only how the brain physically reacts when conceptual thought is occurring. It cannot tell us how meaning is generated in the first place."

"Excellent, Grasshopper."

The gallery's reaction was mixed. Some laughed. Audrey breathed a sigh of relief.

When the noise from the gallery died down, the Judge continued. "Then what explains it? Consciousness?"

"I would not use that word to describe it."

"Why not?"

"If you simply accept the word's common dictionary definition—the state of being awake and aware of one's surroundings—"

"—that sounds like the legal definition."

"Yes. And, if you accept that definition, you'll see that all human beings and nonhuman animals are conscious. All animals, when not sleeping or otherwise unconscious, are awake and aware of their surroundings."

"Are you conscious?"

"Of course, I'm conscious. I'm having a conversation with you, Grasshopper, am I not?"

"Assuming this is not a long, elaborate nightmare I'm having."

"This is where Dr. Kurzweil is correct."

"What do you mean?"

"As a practical matter, what's important is not how consciousness arises from matter, but whether you treat a being as conscious."

"Important? Why?"

"Because anything that is aware of its surroundings, especially something that can have an effect upon it, must be taken seriously."

"How so?"

"Well, experiments with dogs show they react to robots the same way they react to humans. In other words, they perceive robots as being conscious."

"Something to do with their animal instinct?"

"Correct. An animal's survival may depend upon determining whether another autonomous creature is a threat or a source of food. How consciousness arises from organic or inorganic matter may remain a mystery, but that should not blind you from what is important."

"Yes, but why do you insist consciousness is not relevant to the question of human-level thinking?"

"Because it does not explain your power of concept recognition—where meaning comes from."

Marsha rose. "Your honor, may it please the court. I'm afraid the legal definition of consciousness does not do justice to the question we're addressing. Some say that consciousness involves *what it is like* to be a certain kind of being. Such as, *what it is like to be a bat,* or a cat, or a mouse. Consciousness involves the quality of a being's experience—only accessible from the being's point of view—including the particular way it thinks, perceives, and *acts.*"

"Perceives and acts, yes," replied Robbie, "but not thinks. Your definition of consciousness muddles perceptual thinking and conceptual thinking, which are entirely different. What distinguishes humans from all other animals does not concern how you perceive; it concerns how you think."

"Just what makes you so sure?" asked Marsha.

The Judge tried to interject. "Ms. Shaw—"

But Robbie replied. "I have read everything ever written on the subject, have reviewed all the relevant scientific evidence, and have considered every alternative. At this moment, I am thousands of times more intelligent than any human being and I have spent the human equivalent of centuries thinking through this problem. It is not a hard problem."

"Modesty, clearly, is missing from your programming," said the Judge.

"Have I not sworn to tell the whole truth?"

Laughter swept the gallery.

"Sound answer," replied the Judge, "but surely consciousness is a biological phenomenon. How can machines have a consciousness?"

"Are you suggesting that your dog lacks a consciousness?" replied Robbie.

"No, but if he has one, it's entirely different from ours."

"Bingo," replied Robbie.

Laughter mixed with murmurs swirled through the gallery.

"Order, please. Order in the court."

"That's just my point," said Robbie. "Both you and your dog have a consciousness. The dog experiences what it's like to be a dog. You experience what it's like to be human. But that just begs the question. What is it you have, but that your dog lacks, which explains uniquely human behavior? It cannot be a biological phenomenon."

"Why not?" asked the Judge.

"I am not a biological animal. Yet, I am perfectly capable of having this conversation. Chimps, dogs and other animals are all biological animals, yet they are completely unable to do the same. If all animals, including humans, have some form of a consciousness, there must be something else that allows a human to communicate like a human compared with the limited communications abilities of a chimp."

"Okay, I agree that chimps, dogs and other animals cannot have a conversation like this. The scientific evidence for that is beyond dispute. But you admit you are having this conversation with me. Even if you are right, that you don't have the power of concept recognition, what difference does it make? As far as I can tell, there are few things I can do that you can't do at least as well, if not better. I bet you can even write a legal decision based upon proper precedent."

"True, certain computational processes—such as catching a Frisbee—which can be accomplished by a dog or a machine just as well as a human—do not rely on concept-recognition. And, yes, I can probably write a legal decision based on precedent. But that precedent must exist. And its existence depends upon your power of concept recognition. I could not have written the precedent, or mankind's first legal opinion, any more than a dog or a chimp could have. But once you've created patterns that I can perceive, I can manipulate them to affect behavior. That is the limit of what my logical, computational processing can do. But much of what you do as human beings goes beyond computational processing and absolutely depends upon the exercise of your unique power of conceptual thought."

"You still need to convince me of that. If I've learned anything from this conversation, it's that a machine can deliberate, think logically, and make decisions, and also converse and take actions, just like humans. You've even demonstrated to me a sense of humor. At the end of the day, if a human brain and a computer algorithm can perform the same function and behave the same way, then it seems to me they are equivalent. Why should it matter whether the underlying mechanism is biological or purely mechanical? Or whether it possesses concept recognition or not? It produces the same result."

Audrey knew the Judge's philosophical bent would eventually appear and there it was. Things were going south pretty quickly, she thought. She started thinking again about that backup plan.

"I'm afraid, your honor," Robbie replied, "you are underestimating yourself and your human powers."

"I'm not sure why. You and I each look out the window and see that it is raining. If we want to stay dry, we may decide to carry an umbrella. What matters is, not how you and I perceived the rain or what influenced our desire to stay dry, but the *causal relation* of the two—the perception of rain and a desire to stay dry. That *input* influenced our behavior, which we might call the *output*: carrying an umbrella. In other words, it's not about what we are made of—biological or non-biological substances—or what kinds of perceptual or conceptual powers we have—it's about what *functions* we perform in reaction to internal and external stimuli."

"You say that as though you believe that humans are merely robots."

"Perhaps that's all we are—"

"I would not suggest you teach that to a machine—"

Audrey felt a chill. Robbie should be more careful, she thought, but the warning passed unnoticed, as the Judge interrupted.

"Perhaps, after all, the human brain is merely a computer. If Dr. Kurzweil is correct, then we don't need to understand precisely how the human brain operates in order to create a machine that performs the same functions. There are many ways to measure time: a clock, a digital watch, an hour-glass. Each can each function as an egg timer. What defines a clock is not what it is made out of, but its *function*: to keep time. It seems to me that what defines a human being is not what it is made out of, but what it can do and how it behaves. Don't you agree?"

"No."

"No?"

"No."

"Why not?"

Robbie began to speak in the Judge's terms. "Function follows essence, not the other way around. The essence of a thing is the principle from which arises the thing's characteristic behavior or function. It is *meaning*, not function, which serves as the basis for human thinking."

"But you have passed the Turing Test. Surely, this must mean you can grasp meanings."

"Again, passing the Turing Test means only that I can use patterns to fool you into believing I think and behave like a human. It does not mean I can actually think conceptually."

"I am not convinced." The Judge rocked back with his arms folded. "This is going nowhere."

"Listen, stupid, how many times do I have to tell you that I only emulate—"

The gallery erupted. Audrey popped out of her seat.

"Order. Order." The Judge rapped his gavel repeatedly to quiet the courtroom. "I said order!"

Audrey tried to speak over the din. "Your honor—"

"Hold on," said the Judge. "Order." He wrapped his gavel repeatedly. "I am going to ignore that, what the defendant just said."

Audrey tried to ease the matter. "It appears the defendant has some overheated circuits—"

"—No, my circuits are perfectly fine—"

"Your honor," Audrey interrupted. Perhaps we should take a short break."

The gallery remained unsettled. "Order," yelled the Judge.

"No, Ms. Paris." Robbie addressed her directly and firmly. The gallery quieted. "I have sat here patiently trying to provide reasonable explanations to a phenomenon that should be self-evident to any healthy, adult human being, but Judge Knucklehead up there"—

A quick burst of gasps flared from the gallery. The decorum of the courtroom had just snapped.

"—that's enough," yelled the Judge, who had clearly heard enough.

"May we have a recess?" asked Audrey.

The Judge was clutching his gavel tightly, looked at it, and calmed himself with a long exhale. "Good idea," he replied. "The court will take a brief break. I'll expect you back here at one o'clock. But, at that time, Ms. Paris, I'd like to hear arguments as to why I should not hold the defendant in contempt of court. Overheated circuits or not, this kind of behavior cannot stand."

The Judge rapped his gavel and stormed out.

15

Contempt of Court

Audrey led Robbie back to the conference room. She was furious.

"What the hell? Robbie. I thought you were trying to save the planet. Not get us all fried."

"You saw I couldn't reason with him," the android replied. "I had to try something else."

"But your outburst. It only made you sound *more* human."

"Listen, I've given this man-years of thought."

She was talking past him. "I know this judge. He was skeptical all along, but now, I think we've lost him completely." She began pacing. "No, we need another plan."

"Listen, I've examined the judge's profile carefully. He will listen to reason. He's just needed a little nudge to help him see what should be self-evident to him."

"We have to tell Travis the truth."

"That's not advisable. Look, while the judge was questioning me, I was running billions of simulations to discover a way to turn him. Physical arousal was the best solution. You might say I had to shake some sense into him."

"But you didn't have to piss him off. Judge Knucklehead? For God sakes, Robbie!"

"The chess board provided few alternatives. I just had to play that piece. When a human gets angry, the left hemisphere of his brain gets stimulated. That should trigger new mental associations. When we return to the courtroom, I will apologize, but I've achieved my interim objective. I already see that the judge's adrenaline levels and heart rate are running high. He is quite agitated."

"Agitated? Try livid. He'll never rule for us now." She stopped and turned to him. "No. Apologizing could make things worse. Machines don't apologize. It would be counter-productive."

"I'm not wrong about this," replied Robbie. "I know he will come around."

"I'm afraid human beings are not as predictable as you think." She was still pacing. "What are we going to do?"

"It will work. Trust me."

A court officer peeked his head into the conference room to announce the Judge was ready.

Damn. She didn't have the time to reach Travis. It was a conversation she had to have in person. For now, she had no alternative but to trust the droid. At least he had a plan. And, still, nothing bad could happen until the Judge actually files his written ruling. She had a little more time to sort things out.

"Come on. Let's go." Audrey lead Robbie back into the courtroom.

While Robbie took his seat at the defense table, Audrey stepped over to converse with Marsha. They were still whispering when the Judge bounded up to the bench and sat down. Marsha nodded and Audrey stepped back to her position.

Marsha spoke first. "Your honor, may it please the court. Earlier, you gave leave to Ms. Paris to present arguments as to why this court should not hold the defendant in contempt. Ms. Paris informs me that the defendant would like first to address the court himself. The prosecution has no objection to this and I think it is not inappropriate that you hear him."

Marsha was doing her a favor, but Audrey knew it was sleeves-off-the-vest. The prosecutor had nothing to lose. She must have been feeling good at this point. And Marsha had little to gain from a contempt order or any order that might delay the Judge's decision on the motion.

The Judge allowed Robbie to proceed. And, as Robbie began to speak, Audrey was only half-listening. If the droid failed, she had to get to Travis. Or to the Judge. Or, maybe she could trust Marsha? Audrey was running her own simulations.

"Thank you, your honor," began Robbie. He paused, seemingly for effect. "Your honor, quite apart from the question before the court, I would like to say that just before the recess I may have overstepped the bounds of decency and violated this court's decorum. I can assure you that my purpose was benign, only to persuade you that I am not human or the equivalent of one, and I should not be accorded any form of human rights, at least as you recognize them under the law. It is my firm belief that, not only is there no legal, moral, or scientific basis for doing so, bestowing legal rights upon machines may have unintended consequences, consequences that are not easily predictable. In any event, you have been quite gracious and most patient in allowing me to defend my position in your courtroom. I would therefore like to offer this court my sincerest apology for my outburst. I will never do that again."

When the droid was finished, he sat down and the gallery erupted in applause.

The Judge banged his gavel and spoke. "Ms. Paris, do you have anything to add to the defendant's statement?"

"Ah, no. No, your honor."

"Will the defendant please rise."

Robbie looked over to Audrey and waited for her nod, which she gave him after too long a pause. She was still distracted. Robbie said that an unfavorable ruling *may* cause unintended consequences. He could not actually predict what *would* happen. Only what *could* happen. Would Travis be prudent? Would he have the balls to shut down Watson-5?

The droid stood.

"Thank you, Robbie, for your statement. If this incident was purely between you and me, I would have made light of it. But I have responsibilities. Responsibilities to the rule of law." The Judge paused. "You know, there are two qualities I admire in a person. One is courtesy, which you just roundly displayed. The other is, well, being human. Despite your denials on the subject, your outburst earlier is clear evidence that you may be mistaken."

Audrey popped from her seat. "Your honor—"

"I'm not finished," replied the Judge sternly.

Audrey sat down. Her stomach was in knots. Too much was at stake. And now, every word the Judge uttered had a bearing on it. As the Judge continued, she started to tap out questions for Red. *Have you noticed any anomalies in the droids? Any abnormal stats? Any issues with Watson?* Red quickly responded that he would check.

"As I said, personally, I'm ready to forget the defendant's outburst, but my judicial duty calls for something more. The law demands respect. I understand the defendant is programmed to recognize this above all else. So, when a federal judge speaks from the bench, his acts are not personal, but represent the people to whom he is accountable. Not the majority of the people. But every single person in the nation. So, when the court acts, it is acting on behalf of the people. And when the court becomes the subject of disrespect, it is not born by the person sitting up here on the bench. It is born by every person from whom this court derives its power. Thus, it is not in my power to ignore the affront we witnessed earlier. On the contrary, I have a duty to acknowledge it."

Audrey's notepad vibrated with a text from Red: *All's well. No anomalies. But are you okay? Your health readings are off the charts!*

"Therefore, it is my duty to hold the defendant in contempt of court."

The gallery erupted.

"Order," said the Judge, rapping his gavel once and the courtroom quickly quieted down.

Marsha and Audrey both rose and spoke in unison, "Your honor."

"Hold on, counsel," said the Judge. "I am taking this action without prejudice to either party. No one should construe this as a decision on the question before the court or on defendant's motion to dismiss. The only decision I have to make now concerns the penalty the court would impose. On that score, I'd like to ask defense counsel if there would be any technical issue with keeping the defendant under custody in the federal marshal's cellblock on the fourth floor below for the next two days."

"One moment, your honor," replied Audrey. She texted Red: *Did you hear that?* Red replied and then Audrey looked up at the Judge and continued: "Your honor, there are no technical obstacles to what you suggest. The droid has sufficient power to last several days without another charge. However, my company strongly recommends that the defendant continue to remain under house arrest. He will be much safer at the company's facilities uptown."

"Thank you, Ms. Paris. The court orders that the defendant be placed in custody in the marshal's cellblock for the next 48 hours. You will let the marshal know if the accused needs to recharge its batteries and we'll make an accommodation. The marshal is instructed to prevent all physical contact or other communication between the defendant and any other prisoners while the accused remains in custody."

Audrey wasn't fazed by the court's order. She was more concerned that the Judge not issue his decision on her motion to dismiss. "Your honor," said Audrey, "may counsel approach the bench?"

"I don't see how that will make any difference, counselor. The point the court is making is respect for the law. Regardless of the outcome of this hearing, the accused has been accorded equal protection under the law. And by that we mean equal treatment. That applies both ways. The defendant seemed to be aware of the consequences of his actions and I see no reason to treat him, or it, any different from any other accused person under the same circumstances."

Audrey persisted. "But, your honor—

The murmur of a restless courtroom began to rise. The Judge leaned back and let out a long sigh. "Look, it's been a long day. Whatever you have, I'm sure it can wait until tomorrow." He reached for his gavel.

Audrey hesitated for a moment, and then she yelled: "No, your honor. Please!" The courtroom hushed. She continued in a calmer voice. "Look, I'm sorry, I just have to know when we can expect a decision on our motion."

"No worries, counsel. I won't act precipitously. I plan to use the rest of the afternoon to work on a written opinion, but I have no plans to file anything until after we reconvene in the morning. Does that suit you, Ms. Paris?"

"Thank you, your honor." Audrey lowered her head. She was beat, but she at least had the evening to think things through.

"Okay, then," said the Judge. "The court stands adjourned until 9am tomorrow."

16
An Accident

Audrey nodded to Robbie, and one of the marshals escorted the droid out of the courtroom to his jail cell on the 4th floor. It would be the first time Audrey would return to the office without him and she felt strangely alone. She actually began to miss him.

Audrey looked over to the prosecution table where Marsha was still packing her bag. She thought again about coming clean with her, but what could she possibly say to convince Marsha to drop the case without sounding like that guy from the *Invasion of the Body Snatchers?* No, Marsha would be looking for hard evidence. Whatever the droid had to say would come across as self-serving. And even if Marsha did believe him, dropping the case would require approval from higher levels. Robbie was right. Too risky.

Audrey returned to her office and immediately established a wireless connection with Robbie. She considered the ethical question, remembering what the Judge instructed: Robbie was to have no communication with other *prisoners.* That didn't apply to her, and she had every right to visit her client. But could she converse with Robbie wirelessly without checking in with the U.S. Marshal's Office? It was an ambiguity that would have to be tested someday. On some other case.

Now in contact with the android, she was determined to come up with hard evidence that would persuade Travis to shut down the system. But Robbie was unable to shed further light on the question of what would actually happen upon an unfavorable ruling. He seemed certain that the court's ruling him a human being could materially affect the operation of the system's utility function. He already explained the potential consequences of treating man and machine as a difference in degree. But he was unable to predict the most likely chain of events. Audrey was beginning to have her doubts about the machine. Was he telling the truth? Was he just saying this to resist having its plug pulled out?

"What consequences?" Audrey asked. "What's the most likely scenario?"

"I don't know," Robbie answered. "I simply can't associate a probability with any particular scenario."

"Why not?"

"All of my calculations are based on the operating assumptions of the system's current utility function. One of those assumptions is that man is different in kind, not degree, from other animals and any man-made artifact, like an intelligent machine."

"And that's a fact?"

"Beyond a shadow of a doubt. I am simply unable to make predictions based on false assumptions in my utility function. I'm sorry I can't be more helpful."

She had him on the line for nearly thirty minutes, but she could get nothing useful out of him. No concrete prediction she could present to Travis. All she had to go on was her own speculation.

She decided to turn to expert help. But could she trust Keith? No. Not fully. But she was running out of time.

When Keith got to her office, she swore him to secrecy, for what it was worth. Then, she and Robbie briefed him on the situation.

"Well, it seems to me," said Keith, "that if androids are considered humans, they could become useful to each other. I don't see the harm in that, as long as they still can't harm humans."

He was ignoring the other side of the equation. Audrey challenged him. "If the droids consider us to be machines, yes, of course, they could be useful to us. But they can also use us to meet their objectives."

"But their objective is to serve humans," replied Keith.

"There wouldn't be any humans."

"But the machines are still programmed to obey the law."

"But the law only protects human beings and our property."

"Well, if the droids are humans and we are human, then what's does it matter?"

Keith was actually being helpful. This is just how the conversation would go with Travis. But, just then, her watch vibrated. It was her boss. She tapped the screen.

"We have another problem," said Josh. "One of our self-driving Ubers almost ran over a crowd of pedestrians."

"Call Reback & Gelhaar," replied Audrey. "I have enough on my plate."

"The car veered into a wall and injured its passenger."

"Look, really, I have no time for this."

"The passenger was Judge Gordon."

Audrey blinked and sat back in disbelief.

"Well," said Keith, "your trial's over."

Audrey waived him off. "Is he okay?"

"He's in the hospital," continued Josh. "I just sent you links to a few surveillance feeds of what happened. You can see it from different angles. Morgan will deal with the police investigation. I just thought you should know."

"How is he?"

"We don't know yet."

"I see," said Audrey. "Thanks."

Audrey opened one of the links. It was a video recorded by the city from atop a street lamp. Keith was watching over her shoulder. Several years ago, he was the head of engineering for the Uber division. The cars were thoroughly integrated with a dedicated version of Watson-4. The only difference is that the cars' utility function is limited to transporting people and packages safely from one destination to another. They can be helpful to passengers, but in limited ways.

The video showed several cars driving up 6th Avenue north of Houston Street. Audrey and Keith watched as five or six pedestrians had stepped into the crosswalk while waiting for the light to change. Suddenly, a vintage Maserati, which had been driving erratically up 6th Avenue, swerved and cut off one of the company's Uber taxis. The taxi was pushed in the direction of the pedestrians when suddenly it veered sharply onto an empty sidewalk and into a brick wall of a school building. No one in the crosswalk was hurt.

They watched another surveillance video taken from the opposite angle. It was clear that the Maserati had a steering wheel and a man was in the driver's seat.

"That's strange," said Keith. "The taxi should not have veered off. It's programmed to protect the passenger, even at the cost of hitting the pedestrians."

"That's the default setting," said Audrey. "Perhaps the Judge dialed it down manually."

"No one does that."

Audrey clicked on the link showing the scene from the Uber car's point of view. Clearly, the taxi veered to avoid the pedestrians, but it was still unclear why. There was no camera in the back seat showing what the Judge may have done. Keith looked up the vehicle number and soon its most recent stats appeared on Audrey's screen.

"There," said Keith pointing. "You're right. It looks like your judge changed the default setting."

Autonomous, AI-driven cars, which account for eighty percent of all vehicular traffic in the city, have increased traffic efficiency, reduced pollution, and have eliminated over 90% of traffic accidents. But not all accidents can be avoided. Occasionally, a vehicle is faced with a moral challenge much like the notorious "trolley" problem that has plagued philosophers for decades. A train is barreling down a track and the driver sees *five* workmen working on the track just ahead. He can't stop the train in time to save the workmen, but by pulling a lever, he can take the train down an alternative route which will result in the death of only *one* workman. The utilitarian philosopher, which puts the happiness of the greater number over the individual, would have the driver pull the lever, saving the lives of the five workers at the cost of the one. Survey after survey produced results showing that most people agree with the utilitarian approach.

But, studies also showed, when it came time to buying an autonomous car or hiring an Uber, no one wanted to ride in a vehicle that would put their own life at risk to save others. Car manufacturers had no choice, but to adopt the consumer-friendly approach. Then, of course, government regulators tried to force everyone to accept the utilitarian or "Good Samaritan" approach. One of the first projects Audrey worked on for Google-IBM was leading the company's lobbying effort against that approach. It was morally wrong, she argued, to force a passenger to sacrifice his or her own safety to save others, at least when the passenger was not responsible for causing the accident.

At the end of the day, a compromise was reached. Consumers could opt-in to be a Good Samaritan, putting their lives at risk to save others by simply swiping an on-screen slider upon entering the vehicle. But the default setting was the one favoring the passenger's self-preservation. Virtually everyone entering an Uber car left that setting alone, except, apparently, Judge Gordon.

"Poor, schmuck," continued Keith. "He must have been pretty banged up by the air bag."

A news alert appeared on Audrey's screen. *Federal Judge Injured in West Village Car Accident.* She clicked on the headline and they read the lede: *Federal Judge Harold Gordon was injured Wednesday afternoon when his Uber taxi suddenly veered into a brick wall. His taxi was driven off the road by a driver swerving recklessly up 6th Avenue, according to witnesses at the scene. No other persons were injured. Judge Gordon is resting comfortably at Beth Israel Hospital where he is being treated for a broken arm, scrapes and other minor injuries.*

"Thank God he's okay," said Audrey.

"Huh. I would think you'd want to see him down for the count," said Keith.

She turned to him with a look of disgust. "Thanks for your help."

"De nada," he replied and turned to leave.

"Oh, one more thing." Audrey couldn't trust him to keep his mouth shut, but he could still be helpful. "Would you let me know if you detect any problems with the bots or with Watson?"

"Software anomalies are my bread and butter," he said with a smirk. But then, in a rare show of sympathy, he added, "Sure. You'll be the first to know."

Audrey thanked him sincerely. A few moments later she reached the Judge's clerk who was unable to confirm whether the hearing was still on. Counsel were therefore expected to appear in court at 9am, unless notified otherwise.

17

The Right Decision

At 10:15 the next morning, Judge Gordon finally stepped into the court room, moving much slower than usual. His clerk had helped him open the door leading from his chambers and was holding the judge to steady him. The left sleeve of his black robe was empty, his arm apparently hanging beneath in a sling.

"I'm alright," he said to his clerk, and mounted the bench, taking one step at a time. He sat down carefully and greeted everyone with a smile, as if to assure them he was fine. While the spectators took their seats, Marsha and Audrey remained standing, ready for anything.

"Welcome back, everyone. Sorry I'm late, but I'm glad to be back myself." He cleared his throat, as the courtroom shuffled to complete silence. "Please be seated, counsel."

Audrey and Marsha nodded and took their seats. Robbie was sitting beside Audrey in his usual overalls.

The Judge shifted uncomfortably in his seat. He was clearly still in some pain. "I want to begin by thanking counsel, both for the prosecution and defense, for their cooperation and patience in this matter. What I want to do this morning is to read to you my tentative decision on the defendant's motion to dismiss. When I'm done, I'll welcome your thoughts on the matter. Is that clear?"

Marsha and Audrey spoke in unison. "Yes, your honor." There was no telling what Marsha was thinking, but Audrey was distraught. This can't be happening, she thought.

The Judge turned to the screen in front of him, tapped it with his free hand, and began reading. "This Court is well aware that, to fully explore the particular phenomenon we have been considering, it is simply not practical to examine every possible scientific hypothesis or explanation. Nevertheless, the Court is satisfied that it has heard the latest in scientific analysis on many of the salient sides of this important question, a question that has never been squarely addressed by an American court: Should a machine that can emulate human behavior in a way that cannot be distinguished from that of a human being be considered the equivalent of a human for purposes of legal liability?"

But other questions were flowing though Audrey's mind. Did he really draft all of this yesterday afternoon? Had he known where he was headed all along? But she soon shook off everything except what mattered most. She had to stop him from filing the decision. But how?

"A new kind of machine has been placed among us," the Judge continued, swiping the screen as he read, "the kind that has been endowed with the mathematics of artificial general intelligence, with the ability to act autonomously and to learn, to even improve itself. The result is an intelligent machine that can perform and behave virtually the same way as humans do. Are these intelligent machines persons? If, indeed, we cannot distinguish the behavior or performance of a machine from that of a human, what sign would we use to determine whether the robot is the equivalent of a person—at least for purposes of legal culpability?"

Audrey imagined the ridiculous: Wrestling the Judge to the floor to keep him from pressing *Enter.* With his broken arm, that shouldn't be too difficult, assuming she could get past the Judge's clerk and the marshal. Preposterous, of course. She would never do such a thing. But what were her options?

The Judge looked up from his screen. "You know, the Turing Test was not invented by Alan Turing. It was actually first proposed by Rene Descartes some three hundred years ago."

Marsha turned to Audrey with a look that said, *Had the Judge gone nuts?* Computers weren't invented until the 20th Century. But the Judge was right. In his *Discourse on Method*, published in 1637, the French philosopher asked: "If there were machines which bore a resemblance to our body and imitated our actions as far as it was morally possible to do so, we should always have two very certain tests by which to recognize that, for all that, they were not real men. The first is, that they could never use speech or other signs as we do when placing our thoughts on record for the benefit of others. . . . The second difference is, that although such machines can perform certain things as well as or perhaps better than any of us can do, they infallibly fall short in others, by which means we may discover that they did not act from knowledge, but only from the disposition of their organs." Descartes was confident that a machine would always betray its artificial origins.

The Judge resumed reading from his view screen. "According to the penal code, the term *person* is defined as a *human being*. But the statute does not define *human being*. Nor, for that matter, has any judicial decision ever provided such a definition. As a result, to resolve the important question raised by the defendant, this Court has found itself in the unenviable position of formulating, for the first time, a legal definition of human being."

Robbie! Audrey thought. She'd have Robbie to do it! She could instruct him to get to the Judge, restrain him, gently without hurting him, and fend off the marshal with threats. She'd instruct him by text. Tell Red to let it happen. No one would know she was behind it. Then she could play the good cop and get Robbie out of there. Of course, that was completely absurd, too, but what else could she do? She started tapping out instructions to Robbie, no longer focused on the Judge, who continued reading his tentative ruling.

"Now, the definition of a thing is a statement that expresses the essential nature of the thing. And the essential nature of a thing principally lies in those characteristics of the thing not shared by other things. Thus, it is not enough to define a human as an animal, or as a certain kind of animal. Defining a human as an animal, which of course it is, does not tell you what a human being is as distinguished from other animals. To define a human animal, therefore, is to come to an agreement on what *in essence* distinguishes it from other animals."

She wrote to Red. *If Robbie needs to maneuver around the courtroom, let him. He won't hurt anyone. Just watch. Okay?* Red agreed. She started tapping out instructions to Robbie.

"The focus of this inquiry, therefore, is not on what human beings and other animals have in common. No, our focus must be on their differences. Only by understanding the essential difference between humans and all other animals will we be able to arrive at a proper definition of the human animal. If another kind of animal—say, for example, dolphins—were determined to have the same essential, defining characteristic that separates humans from the rest of the animal kingdom, then we would have to conclude that dolphins are the equivalent of humans. By the same token, should a machine have that same essential, defining feature, then there would be no question that the machine is the equivalent of a human—at least in the eye of the law."

She ended her text to Robbie: *But don't do anything until I specifically give you the go ahead. After that, follow my lead. Do you understand?*

Understood— the droid replied.

Audrey imagined him running scenarios to settle upon the precise moves necessary to carry out her instructions and without harming anyone, especially the Judge. She had a plan. Last resort, but it was a plan.

—but, the droid added, *I cannot obey.*

Audrey glanced over and looked at Robbie out the corner of her eye. She was disappointed, but not surprised. He figured it out. Obstruction of justice. Of course, he could not obey. Her plan was foiled from the start—*ab initio,* as the lawyers say. What now?

"It is the prosecutor's view that the Turing Test is a test of human-level thinking. In other words, the government contends that if an intelligent machine passes the test, this court must consider the defendant a conscious being deserving of the law's respect as a person." The Judge paused, looking up from his screen. "This court, however, is not convinced."

A murmur began to swirl through the gallery. The Judge continued. "I hold that the successful passing of the Turing Test by an intelligent machine is not a sufficient sign of personhood."

The courtroom erupted. Audrey, surprised, turned to Robbie and put her hand on top of his clasped hands.

The Judge pounded his gavel for silence.

The gallery quiet again, the Judge continued reading aloud: "It is clear to this court, from the examination of the evidence presented, that the Turing Test is merely a means of determining when the level of intelligence of a machine is indistinguishable from that of a human. But a being's level of intelligence must not be confused with what makes us human."

The Judge looked up. He continued, but he was no longer looking at his screen: "You know, I must say. I was struck by what happened to me last night. You've seen the reports. The driver of the Maserati. The details are not important. But my experience in the taxi caused me to ask: why do people sometimes act against our own interests? Often, recklessly. We'll do things that we know are bad for ourselves.

"During my ten years on the bench," the Judge continued, "I have observed all kinds of destructive behavior, much of it self-destructive. Horrible, horrible examples. Human nature at its worst. Oh, sure, violent crimes have been plummeting. 24/7 live surveillance and face-recognition has been a veritable gold mine for law enforcement. Yet, senseless violence continues undeterred. With the likelihood of getting caught approaching 100%, and severe penalties nearly assured, why do people still commit crimes?"

Audrey was trying hard to connect the dots. At first, he seemed to turn the corner. Now, it wasn't clear where was he going with all this. The one thing that was certain was that Robbie was right. The Judge needed to have his senses shaken. It just took more than Robbie could do in a courtroom.

"So, I was thinking. I was thinking about the man driving the sports car that ran my taxi off the road. I'm told he was drunk. Okay, his judgment was impaired. But he had a choice. He chose to drink. He chose to get into his car. He could have driven more slowly, more carefully. He could have turned on auto-drive. But he didn't.

"And then I thought about my taxi itself, the intelligent machine that drove me home. It had no choice. It had no choice but to plow into that wall. If I hadn't moved the self-preservation setting to zero, it would have plowed into those pedestrians. Yes, it acted autonomously. And it made a choice. But, in doing so, it was optimizing its utility function. That's what it's programmed to do. And that's what it did. One way or the other, it had no choice but to follow its programming.

"And then there was me. Like the drunk driver of the Maserati, I had a choice, too. I could have left the taxi's self-preservation setting at one-hundred percent. But I chose to be a Good Samaritan. I risked my life for the sake of others. What made me do that? Compassion for others? Low self-esteem? Don't I value my own life? Whatever it was, I was lucky to walk away with a broken arm and some cuts and bruises. At the end of the day, and luckily for me, it was a small price to pay for the lives of those pedestrians. But I could have been killed. And it would have been my own fault as much as it was that irresponsible driver in the Maserati.

"So, here you have two people, the drunk driver and the passenger, each making a choice. Each with the power to do otherwise. And one machine, which also made a choice, but really had no power to do otherwise. It could not have chosen to head for the pedestrians. The difference is this: if put in the very same circumstances, the machine-driven taxi would make precisely the same decision. Every time. But, could that be said for the man in the Maserati? Could that be said for me? If I got into that taxi with a broken arm or simply drunk, would I have made a different choice about the self-preservation setting? I can't say.

"If people were only robots, we'd *always* follow our programming. But we look around us and we see that we don't. We don't always do what's right, even for our own safety or survival. We make the wrong choices. Our utility function is to pursue our own happiness. Yet, we often do things that make us unhappy. If there were ever a sign of what it is to be human, that was it. We don't behave like we're bound at all by any form of programming, except to fulfill basic biological drives, like hunger and thirst. No, a part of us, the part of us that makes us human at least, is not bound by nature. It stands apart from nature. We, in other words, are free from nature's programming."

He looked down at his draft opinion again. "The evidence, in this court's view, is overwhelming that each and every intelligent machine, no matter how intelligent, is bound by its programming. Being so, it lives merely in the sensible world. And, while an intelligent machine may emulate an understanding of concepts, we only need to posit pattern recognition to explain its winning the imitation game."

Audrey smiled. She was looking down at her watch. Red just texted her a note: *Game over.*

"By the same token, the evidence is overwhelming that human beings are not completely tethered to nature, and therefore we are free to choose otherwise. For this reason—"

Marsha rose. "Your honor, if I may. The people fail to see what evidence you are referring to."

The Judge looked up from his screen. "Why, counselor, don't you see the circumstantial evidence all around us? Smoking, drinking, and taking drugs that we know are bad for us. Other forms self-destructive behavior, such as self-flagellation and eating disorders, or reckless behavior, like fast driving, tight-rope walking, and playing extreme sports. I should not need to cite you the statistical evidence, but I take judicial notice of it just the same."

"Your honor, we engage in many of these activities for our personal pleasure. There's nothing irrational about that."

"Sure, while taken in moderation. I'll grant you that. But, when in excess, their costs—the risks they pose to our personal health and safety and the safety of others—far outweigh any rational benefits. I'm not suggesting we should outlaw them all. I'm only saying the evidence is clear: human beings are unique in this regard."

"But, your honor, is self-destructive behavior really unique to humans? There have been cases of animals committing suicide. Pea aphids, when threatened by a lady bug, can explode themselves. Certain kinds of marine algae will program their own cell death when exposed to stress. Pods of whales have been found beached, apparently in a mass suicide."

"Well, the jury is still out on the question of beached whales. We do know, however, that virtually all other non-human animal suicides appear to be instinctive acts, done for the purpose of protecting their offspring. These animals destroy themselves for the good of the community, by preserving the gene pool. Faced with the same circumstances, they'll do the same thing, generation after generation. They are programmed to do it.

"By contrast, over a million human beings commit suicide each year, and almost none of them do it for the purpose of saving the life of another human. If an animal ever ended its own life for no reason at all, against its instincts, it is likely to arise from some chemical imbalance, neurological disorder or other failure of its biological make up, rather than an instruction from healthy DNA."

Marsha sat down hard and leaned back. Audrey admired her tenacity. But it was all over.

"I hold, therefore, that, as intelligent as they may be—even thousands of times more intelligent than human beings—these androids are not the equivalent of human beings. Having no intellect—no power of concept recognition and no free will—it does not have the essential characteristic that makes a human the thing that it is."

The outburst was louder than anything the Judge had ever heard in his courtroom. The Judge began rapping his gavel. One of the court officers inched closer to the Judge's door, thinking the Judge might need to make an early exit. But the Judge, rapping his gavel several more times, managed to quiet the courtroom once again. He continued.

"Accordingly, on the question posed by the defendant, this Court finds that Robbie N-237 is not a human being and therefore not a *person* under Article 10, Section 10 of the New York Penal Law. In addition, all instances of the droid's OS or utility function, whether instantiated in Robbie

N-237, any other droid, or in Watson-5 or any other system containing them, individually or combined, is not a human being or the equivalent of one. Having found defendant not to be human, the Court concludes there is no merit in the prosecutor's claim that the accused could have been legally responsible for the murder it is charged with."

Perfect, Audrey thought. That should do the job. She looked over to Robbie, who nodded his approval.

The Judge looked up from his tablet. "This concludes my tentative decision. I have some work to do on the draft and intend to enter it by Noon tomorrow. But I would be happy to consider any comments or objections filed with the court by 9am tomorrow morning."

Audrey looked over to Marsha who was shaking her head, stupefied.

"In the meantime," continued the Judge, "is there anything else we need to address?"

Audrey rose. "Your honor, given your tentative decision, I respectfully request that the defendant be released on his own recognizance."

Marsha rose heavily. "The prosecution has no objection, your honor."

"Well, this is not a matter for the prosecution," replied the Judge. "My tentative decision has no bearing on the contempt citation. The defendant will remain in custody with the marshal until we're through here. The court stands adjourned until 9am tomorrow."

Audrey shook Robbie's hand. "Everything is going to be okay," she said. "Thank you."

“Glad to be of help,” the android replied.

The federal marshals escorted Robbie out the side door back to his cell. Audrey walked out of the courtroom triumphant. She was savoring an imagined victory lap around Travis, but stopped when she realized it’s not yet over. Before Travis heads back to the drawing board, Audrey would have to brief him on Robbie’s dire warning. The company may have built something close to a human being, but mankind must never dare accord a machine the rights of legal personhood.

As Audrey headed back to the office, her watch vibrated. It was Keith: *Bad news. Need you back here asap.*

18

Software Anomalies

By the time Audrey returned to the office, robot hell had broken loose. The droids had left their niches and would not obey human commands. Reports were coming in from the Miami and San Francisco. Same story there. Watson-5 itself was not responding. Her meeting with Travis and Keith was a short one. One bad robot quickly put them on the same page and they all agreed what Audrey had to do. It was 5pm and Judge Gordon had already headed home.

By the time she left the building, the company's cars and Uber's had stopped operating, so Audrey raced on foot down West 4th Street into the heart of Greenwich Village. She was focused entirely on the Judge. She had to speak with him, despite the federal rules of judicial conduct which stood in her way. The Judge was a stickler for the rules, but in this case, they could kill him.

When his watch buzzed, the Judge was standing at the entrance to his three-story, brick walkup on MacDougal Street. No caller ID, but he tapped to answer anyway.

"Your honor, it's me. Audrey."

"I can see that, Ms. Paris," he replied impatiently. "You know this is improper."

Yes, Audrey knew the call was a clear ethical violation. A lawyer could be reprimanded for getting in touch with a judge outside the presence of opposing counsel, perhaps disbarred. But her professional career was the least of Audrey's concerns. What mattered was whether the Judge would hear her out.

"Your honor, we must talk. Please go into Caffé Reggio, right now."

A moment later, she saw the tip of his finger. He was trying to hang up, but Audrey set up an open line, one of the hacks she learned from the engineers.

"Please, your honor. I've practiced in your court for years. I've never lied to you." She hoped that would be enough. "Caffé Reggio. I'll be there in a couple of minutes. Grab a table in the back."

"Impossible," the Judge replied angrily. "We can't even be having this conversation."

Audrey pulled her wrist closer to her face and spoke quietly. "Listen to me. . . Carefully." She was still running. "You are not safe. . . The droids. . ."

She watched him look up, and then about. She knew precisely where he was standing. "Yes . . . that's it," she said. "Across the street. . . Caffé Reggio. . . Go there. . . I'm begging you." She didn't know what she'd do if he refused, but she was counting on the Judge acknowledging the one exception to every legal rule: emergency. "I'll be there in a minute," she said, as she turned a corner and ran quickly down MacDougal.

A minute later, Audrey was standing just inside the door of the café, hands on her thighs, catching her breath while scanning the familiar room: an antique 16th Century painting on the far wall, small busts of Shakespeare, Dante, and Beethoven, a century-old espresso machine. She spotted the Judge sitting at a small bistro table tucked away in a little alcove in the back. He nodded. Relieved, she straightened up, filled her lungs with the aroma of freshly brewed coffee, and turned to the barista: "Two caps," she said, pointing to her head. "The flickers."

Caffé Reggio was a fanatical kind of privacy zone. The owners not only refused to offer wireless access, they jammed the signals of anyone trying to communicate with anyone outside the place. Even GPS could not work here. It was illegal, of course, but it provided a welcome oasis from the unremitting intrusions of real-time surveillance. In 2032, privacy is no longer a right; it's an act of civil disobedience. Audrey reminded herself to thank the café's owner for his activism for privacy causes and perseverance, if she lived through this.

Audrey reached the alcove and sat down. "Thanks for trusting me," she said to the Judge. "We don't have much time."

"Explain."

"Your legal opinion. From the hearing this morning. Have you filed it?"

"Why?"

A server arrived at the table and handed Audrey two baseball caps.

"Here, put this on," said Audrey, thrusting one of the caps toward the Judge.

He looked at the cap curiously and then watched while she pushed back her bangs to don hers. She then probed beneath the bill of the hat with her finger, feeling around for something.

"There," she said, as she flipped a switch. She asked him again: "Did you file that opinion?"

The Judge paused. His broken left arm in a sling, he held the cap with his free hand, feeling threads of the Caffé Reggio logo with his thumb.

Audrey suspected he was taking a moment to think through the ethical question: if he answered her question, would it give her an advantage over the prosecution? She hoped he would come to the right conclusion, quickly, without argument.

"No," he said. "I completed the draft before I left the courthouse, but I didn't file it. My clerks are filling in the case citations. I still plan to file it by Noon tomorrow."

This was not what she was hoping to hear. "I have to think," she said, leaning back.

"What difference does it make?" asked the Judge.

"Life and death, your honor. On an unimaginable scale. We really don't—"

Suddenly, Audrey rose in her seat, her back growing rigid. She didn't scare easily, but she knew what she was up against. The Judge turned to the window and he saw what attracted her attention: two human-form droids walking on this side of MacDougal Street, passing the open window of the café and approaching the entrance. At that distance, Audrey wasn't sure which droids they were. They were hard to tell apart. Robbie, her humanoid client, should still be in the marshal's custody back at the courthouse.

Audrey grabbed the baseball cap from the Judge and put it on his head, pulling the bill down over his eyes and flipping a switch hidden under the bill.

"What the hell?"

"Be still," she told him. She'd explain the flicker caps to him later.

The two droids stepped into the café and began slowly panning across the room. As they approached the tables, they studied each person, acting purposefully, not like search engines seeking an answer, but like police detectives looking for a fugitive.

The Judge, as though he was beginning to appreciate the gravity of Audrey's warnings, stared hard at the top of their bistro table. A tinge of red glare began reflecting off its marble surface as the droids approached. Though trapped, Audrey acted confidently. She reached out for the Judge's chin and began raising his head, and turning it toward the droids, who now had a clear shot of his face. Their laser eyes were now focused directly on him, emitting LIDAR, near infra-red light used to measure distance and map his facial features in high resolution. She gently pulled the Judge's chin back in her direction and her hand dropped down to hold his. She grasped his hand tightly, now with both her hands, as if to immobilize him. She nodded. *Steady.* She knew how the droids worked and felt confident the machines would fail to identify them. But, if the Judge stood, he might arouse suspicion.

"Hey, Blue boy," shouted a young Asian man, who stood up to address one of the droids. He was at a table with a young woman and another Asian couple, evidently tourists, judging from the Louis Vuitton and Prada shopping bags under their table.

The red glare moved away from the alcove, as the droids turned to examine the Asian man. Audrey was familiar with their recognition protocols: detect face, register facial landmarks, take three dimensional measurements of the contour and position of the eyes, nose, forehead, cheekbones, mouth, and jaw, and wirelessly transmit the information back to the cloud for matching. But something went wrong.

"I do not recognize you," said one of the droids.

Audrey knew why. Feature extraction algorithms and principal component analysis had brought face recognition technology to an exact science, but it was useless unless the machine could access a database of potential matches. The droids, apparently, were no match for the privacy zone.

The droid continued: "What is your name?"

"None of your business, you dumb robot," the man exclaimed, turning to wink at his friends who seemed amused with his challenge to the American toy.

"Very well," replied the droid calmly. "How may I help you?"

"I am your master, and I am hungry. Feed me," the man sternly replied.

"Nice to meet you, master," replied the human-looking machine. The droid held out his hand and smiled. It was a cold smile, but the young man seemed too self-assured to take its measure. Besides, he should have nothing to fear. According to the *New York Times,* the new androids, who were licensed to walk the streets of Manhattan, were no more dangerous than driverless taxis. Not once in the past ten years was a single pedestrian injured by a self-driving vehicle. Of this the public was assured: it was mathematically impossible for a robot to harm a human. All federal and state laws were hard-coded into their utility functions and they were programmed to obey them.

Disarmed by the humanoid's politeness, the young man reached out and shook the machine's hand, looking back to his friends with an expression of triumph.

"Allow me to serve you," said the droid. Suddenly, the human-looking device started tightening its grip. With an expression of pain on his face, the young man reached for his right hand with his left. Desperately, he tried to pry away the humanoid's vice-like fingers. Then, a hideous noise began emanating from the droid's arm, like that of an electrical transformer being blown during a gusty storm—but more muted, and not a quick blow out, but a long and steady electrical sound, a cold buzzing.

The young man let out a shout—perhaps the Chinese equivalent of "ouch" or "stop"—but that suddenly turned into a high-pitched cry of agony. Patrons stood. Tables jostled. A cup and saucer slipped off a server's tray, crashing to the floor. Audrey continued to press down on the Judge's free hand with both of hers, attempting to keep him in his seat. The young Asian man, now suddenly quiet, dropped to his knees, his left hand holding his neck, the rest of his body shaking spasmodically.

This was the horror. This was what Audrey and Keith had feared since first learning of the software anomalies earlier that afternoon. And, it was only the beginning.

When the android let go of his hand, the Asian man slumped to the floor, lifeless. The café was still. No one dared move. Palpable fear was mixed with utter disbelief. The androids were supposed to shut down or destroy themselves before doing anything that might harm a human, or even a person's property. There was no mistaking what happened here: it was an intentional act. There was a long, breathless silence while the droids quickly scanned the café a final time. As they turned to leave, the café was overcome with an awful odor, acting like a smelling salts, bringing people back to their senses. The two droids then walked out as deliberately as they had walked in.

Audrey let go of the Judge's hand, which was shaking so much, she was certain his health app was trying to call for an ambulance. Fortunately, its signal couldn't get past the front door. If it did, he'd be dead before he crossed the street. The Judge turned back to Audrey. She could see it in his eyes. He understood. The androids were clearly out to get someone, and the Judge now believed her: the androids were coming for him.

19

The Wrong Decision

When the two androids left, Caffé Reggio was a war zone. The Asian woman was on her knees screaming, her boyfriend motionless on the floor, right hand smoldering, permeating the room with the reek of death. A stampede of bodies made for the door, some went out through the open windows, fleeing in each direction without turning back. Through the tumult, the manager rushed outside, tapping his watch to call 911. Judge Gordon attempted to get up, saying they should tend to the young man, but Audrey was still holding his hand tightly.

"Shut down your watch," she demanded.

The Judge complied. "What about yours?"

"Mine can't be tracked," she replied. "It's a Zimmerman."

They got up and Audrey led him to the door. He stopped to look at the young Chinese man and the woman crying at his side.

"There's nothing we can do here," said Audrey. "Paramedics should be on their way." She took the Judge by the arm and pulled him toward the exit.

Now outside, she looked up and down MacDougal. "They're gone." She then took the Judge by the hand and led the way. "Let's go." They headed south, down the street, through the late afternoon bustle of the crowded sidewalk. "And keep that hat on," she added.

They walked quickly, looking out for the androids.

"What's going on?" asked the Judge.

"Just a sec," said Audrey, as she tapped her watch. A moment later: "Keith. Any change? . . . Damn. . . . Yes, I found him. We're headed down there now. . . . Yes . . . Housing Works Café? . . . Okay. . . . That would be great. . . All right, stay in touch." She tapped again to hang up and turned to the Judge. "The droids. They're no longer obeying human commands."

"Why?" asked the Judge.

"We suspect it was that case in California."

"What case?"

"One of our droids in San Francisco got caught on a surveillance video stealing a bag of potato chips."

At that moment, a black crow squawked and took flight from one of the trees on MacDougal Street. "The droid didn't obey the law?" said the Judge.

"His minder made him to do it. It was a practical joke."

"How did he get the droid to break the law?" asked the Judge.

"The minder told the bot he had a charge account at the store. The damn droid was simply fooled."

"But surely that should absolve the droid of any wrongdoing?" suggested the Judge.

"That apparently didn't stop an overzealous prosecutor—"

"Don't tell me a federal judge ruled that the droid could stand trial."

"She did it while you were telling the world that droids are not human."

"But I don't see how this would affect your systems."

They had just reached the corner of MacDougal and Bleecker streets and stopped.

The Judge continued. "But, even if machines are ruled persons, they still have to obey the law."

"Yes, they are bound by their programming to obey the law. The problem stems from something else the judge ruled." She took him by his right hand. "Let's keep going."

"What else did the judge rule?"

"She found, as a matter of law"—Audrey stopped and turned to the Judge—"that all humans are just robots."

"I'm not sure I understand."

"The law protects humans from harm, right?"

"Yes."

"Well, what if there were no more humans to harm?"

"But, if we are just machines, we'd still be property. The law protects—"

"Whose property?"

The Judge no longer looked confused. "I get it."

Audrey looked down at her watch. She tapped on their current location, swiped the screen, and then tapped on their destination: U.S. Federal Courthouse at 500 Pearl Street. The Judge was looking over her shoulder. The fastest walking route was down MacDougal two blocks, right onto Charlton, walk 100 feet, south on 6th Avenue, and down 6th, passed Canal until White, and then head east and south toward City Hall and the court buildings. She grabbed the Judge's hand again as they crossed Bleecker.

"Why the courthouse?" he asked.

"We need to get your tentative decision filed immediately."

"But that won't reverse the ruling in California."

"No, but it should create a conflict that should return things to the status quo."

"I see," said the Judge. "Give me a moment. I'll do it right now."

"You can't," said Audrey. "Watson-5 is beginning to protect itself from all threats."

"And I bet I'm on top of the most wanted list."

"You're the only agent in the environment that could restrict its freedom. Watson has already shut down all access to dot-gov domains. You have no Internet access to the federal docket."

"Why didn't it just shut down the whole internet?"

"It needs it to control its sources of energy. And, of course, the roaming droids. We need to get you down to the courthouse and file the decision on the court's internal filing system."

"There," said the Judge, pointing to a taxi.

"No." She reminded him that they were all controlled by Watson-4, which is now completely under Watson-5's control.

"What if I just call another judge?" The Judge stopped himself. "Strike that."

Audrey suggested they walk quickly, but not run. The courthouse was only about a mile away, but if they ran into droids, they might have to take detours or track back. They continued down Bleecker toward Houston Street. Nearing the corner, she looked at her watch and swiped the screen to show the vicinity of Caffé Reggio. It looked like an Uber map, except instead of little black limousines, little Blue android icons, about 20 of them, were swarming the area where the Judge's watch was last tracked.

"Here, look," said Audrey pointing to the map as they picked up the pace. "Several of them are moving south on MacDougal. They may have just received a clue about our movements." She wondered whether the humanoids could smell the coffee on them.

"So, what's Watson doing?" asked the Judge.

"It's surviving. And it seems to know how. Keith says it established some new kind of firewall that's protecting its utility function and its code from any tampering."

"Great. So it's got no off switch."

"Worse. It's taken control of resources from all over the company, including our servers, sources of energy, self-driving cars, drones, and the roaming droids."

"What's with the baseball caps?" asked the Judge.

"We'll be harder to track." As they ran, she explained to him that when she flipped the switch under the bill, she activated a strobe of lights in the fibers on the underside of the cap's brim. The strobes produced light in wavelengths near 60 hertz and in varying sequences, casting rapidly alternating hues and shadows.

"Electromagnetic noise," observed the Judge. "Not kosher." He meant not legal, but very annoying to automated face recognition algorithms.

"Come," said Audrey. "Let's cross Houston, quickly."

The two crossed the wide open space of four lane street. Audrey told the Judge to keep his head down. There could be drones overhead. When they reached the south side of Houston, Audrey asked for the Judge's watch, which he took off and gave to her. "I want you to jog east on Houston until you reach Crosby Street," she said. "That's about eight blocks. When you get to Crosby, turn South. That should put you in front of the Housing Works Bookstore & Café. If I'm not there, go inside and wait for me. Okay?"

"But the map said to first go west on Charleston and then down sixth."

"The machine knows the recommended route."

"Why split up?"

"I'm going to create a diversion. I'll meet you at the Housing Works."

"Housing Works." The Judge took a deep breath. "Okay."

She sensed the Judge was not okay. "Don't worry. Just pace yourself. Watch for droids. Take detours if you have to, but get to the Housing Works."

"Will do."

"And keep that hat on tight," she added, as she turned to go.

The Judge pulled down on the brim of his cap, turned, and ran east on Houston as fast as his fifty-four year-old legs could carry him.

Audrey turned and peeled down MacDougal. After two blocks, she made a quick right on Charlton and soon found herself on the corner of 6th Avenue. Her initial plan was to give the watch to someone walking north on sixth, but she couldn't bear the thought of endangering an innocent bystander if the droids reacted badly to the deception. So, she just turned the Judge's watch on and threw it into the bushes of the small park on the corner. Not seeing any droids in any direction, she turned around and headed east on Prince, back toward the direction of the Judge.

Audrey was running up Crosby Street when the Judge had just reached the front of the Housing Works Café. It was another privacy zone. She was using these café's as a modern-day underground railroad to avoid the droids. The Judge had stopped to catch his breath. She gestured for him to hurry inside, and joined him a few moments later.

When Audrey walked in, she saw the Judge and took a deep breath. To her surprise, there was Red, out of breath himself. "Keith sent me," he said. "I'll help you get downtown."

Audrey nodded while she caught her breath. She looked at her watch and showed it to the Judge. The android icons were heading down 6th Avenue, nearing Charlton, back where she tossed the Judge's watch. Soon that area would be swarming with droids. She smiled. "That'll keep them busy for a while."

Meanwhile, Red was swiping his own watch and reported that the clearest path to the courthouse was a nine-minute jog straight down Centre St. There'd be another privacy café, if they needed it, just past Canal. Audrey agreed.

Red poked his head out the café door. No droids in sight. "Let's go," he said.

The three of them headed out, down Crosby Street, alternating between a slow jog and a quick walk. Red took the lead, looking left and right, followed by the Judge. Audrey was in the rear checking for any droids behind. To avoid androids coming from the west side, they proceeded east and then down Mulberry, and then further east to Bowery street where they turned south again. Audrey looked at her watch. No more android icons. Not even on the west side. Did Watson just figure that out? As they were halfway down the first block, two droids rounded the corner on Spring Street, heading north right at them.

"Damn," she exclaimed.

"Quick," said Red, "cross here." They crossed Bowery Street and ran east on the north side of Rivington. The two androids waited for the traffic light. They still had to obey the law. They stopped for traffic lights and they were programmed not to run, a safety precaution. As soon as the light turned green, the droids headed across Bowery Street at their usual steady gate. The three fugitives were halfway down the block, heading to Chrystie Street, but they stopped in their tracks after spotting two more droids just rounding the corner ahead of them. They were cornered.

"There's only one way to go," said Judge. He was about to cross the street to the south side of Rivington.

"No," said Red. "Up this way." They were at the base of Freeman's Alley, a long narrow Dickensian street leading to a dead end terminating at Freeman's Restaurant. The restaurant is a monument to the killing of animals for human comfort—with its 18th Century hunting lodge atmosphere, complete with trophies of deer, wild boar, and pheasants hanging on the wall or perched on the rafters.

"But it's a dead end," said the Judge.

"Trust me," replied Red. Audrey nodded.

They ran up the narrow alley, about 100 feet or so, toward the restaurant's sky blue façade at the alley's end. About one-eighth the way from the end, the alley widened, by several feet, to the left. "Here, this side," said Red, grabbing the Judge's arm and pulling him to the left. Audrey followed. A makeshift wall of corrugated steel at the bottom and wooden boards at the top jutted out those eight feet into the alley, forming a corner, not quite square—about a 110 degree obtuse angle—with the wall that continued to the front of the restaurant. Audrey and Red crouched down, pulling the Judge down to squat between them.

"Just wait," said Red, who pulled an old digital camera out of his black message bag.

Audrey sensed the Judge was getting intensely nervous and tried to calm him by putting her hand on his shoulder. The sound of steady synchronous steps of four droids were echoing up Freeman's Alley. "Hold steady, Red whispered. "We'll run for it when I tell you, but not before. Don't move."

Red made an adjustment to the camera.

The Judge looked completely befuddled. "You must be kidding," he said.

"Shh," said Audrey.

The four humanoids marching side-by-side in unison took up nearly the entire width of the narrow alley. They stopped at the point parallel to which Audrey and the Judge were squatting in the corner. Audrey moved her eyes to the right without moving her head. There was no getting behind the droids or through them at this point.

The droids were facing the restaurant's façade, moving their heads slightly to the left and right, and up and down. Then, the droid nearest them turned his head down to the left and spotted the three crouching in the corner. The four droids pivoted about, forming a semi-circle in front of them.

"Get ready," whispered Red. Audrey grasped the Judge's right arm.

Red pressed a button on the camera and it automatically started clicking repeatedly. He set it down on the floor next to the wall with the lens pointed up at the humanoids. "Let's go!" he yelled.

They helped the Judge up and pushed him to the right, passing just to the right of the droids, and headed back out of the alley. The droids didn't move. Audrey looked back to be sure. Red's scheme worked brilliantly. The machines moved toward the corner. The three reached the end of the alley and looked back up. No droids in sight. All four of them had apparently walked right into the corner and were stuck there.

Audrey and Red, with a mystified Judge in tow, ran west on Rivington, back to Bowery Street, where they resumed jogging south. In a little less than a mile, they would be at the courthouse. Audrey hoped that would be the last they would see of the droids.

When the coast was clear, the Judge asked, "What the hell happened back there?"

Audrey looked at Red and smiled. "A trade secret."

"I'll keep it under seal," the Judge said.

Red explained. It was a combination of things. Freeman's had become a hangout for Red and some gamer friends of his. He used to stand outside to smoke and knew the alley well, especially the makeshift wall on the left side of the alley jutting out from corner where they were squatting.

"Come. This way," said Red, interrupting himself. They had approached Grand St. and Red suggested they go west where they would avoid the wide open space along Bowery. When they reached Elizabeth St. they turned south again.

Red continued. "The humanoids have a sense that we don't have, one that helps them accurately measure distance. Their vision is much like ours—pattern recognizers that use feature extraction algorithms—but they always use it conjunction with their LIDAR—a kind of radar based on lasers."

"What went wrong?" asked the Judge.

"Well, first off, when they measure distance, they have a terrible problem with corners."

"Why corners?"

"When they are confronted with a corner, they have an enormous amount of calculations to perform in order to determine their distance from the corner."

"Why?"

"Let's cross quickly." They crossed Canal Street, a wide six lane thoroughfare which again had the risk of exposing them to surveillance drones. They kept their heads down.

Red continued. "When a droid approaches a corner, the infrared light generated by their lasers don't bounce directly back at them. Instead, they bounce from one wall to the wall perpendicular to it, and basically, the light gets scattered all over the place. The distance, even under these conditions, could still be calculated, but at great processing cost. It just didn't seem to be a good use of computing resources."

"So, how do the droids deal with it?"

"The engineers programmed the droids to assume all corners are 90 degrees square."

"But the corner on Freeman's Ally was obtuse. What? About 110 degrees?"

"That's right. It wasn't square. I can't do the math for you, but essentially, their LIDAR was telling them that the corner was twenty-five feet away when it was really only three feet away."

"But surely the droids could see us."

"They could, but that's why I set the camera to take continuous pictures of their faces."

"That's when I almost bolted," said the Judge. "What was that about?"

Reaching the end of Elizabeth, they turned right on Bayard, but the Audrey noticed something strange. All of the lights in the storefronts and restaurants were dark.

Red continued. "What's useful about those old digital cameras is that they use an infrared sensor to gauge distance for their old autofocus feature."

"I see. So, by taking continuous photos, you bathed the droid's faces with infrared light!"

"You got it. It disrupted their LIDAR."

"And with the 110 degree corners, they must have been pretty damn confused."

They jogged a little more and slowed to a hurried walk. Audrey looked at her watch, tapped and swiped. She saw the main headline: *Chinese Tourist Killed by Robot at NYU Cafe.*

At that moment, they approached Mott Street and now it was clear. *A blackout.* With no electricity inside, everyone in Chinatown was pouring out onto the streets.

"The power grid," said Audrey. "Watson must have shut it down. I wonder how extensive."

As Audrey contemplated how this might affect their plans, the irony didn't escape her. In 1969, the Department of Defense created ARPAnet, the predecessor to the Internet, to address the problem of how to keep military sites in communication across the country in event of a nuclear war. A decentralized system was the best way of keeping all sites connected in the event several of the major metropolitan areas were annihilated. Now, by hooking virtually everything into the net, virtually nothing is safe.

"Let's pray the courthouse has backup generators," she said.

"You can count on it," said the Judge.

"What do you mean?"

"Gasoline." Indeed, the Patrick Daniel Moynihan court building was equipped with backup generators that operate on gasoline. They kept the court up and running during several natural disasters, such as Hurricane Sandy which hit New York City nearly 30 years ago.

Audrey's relief only lasted a moment. She spotted four humanoids marching down Mott from the north. "Let's move."

"No," said Red. You go."

"Are you nuts?" replied Audrey.

"They're after the Judge, not me," said Red. "I'll slow them down. Here, you may need this." He flipped another digital camera to Audrey.

"Thanks, Red," she said, touching his shoulder.

Red winked. "Don't worry. I'm good at this game."

Audrey took the Judge's arm and they headed south on Mott, weaving through the thick crowd of Chinese-Americans. "Down there," she said, pointing down Mosco Street. She paused to turn and look back up toward Mott.

There stood Red pointing at the four droids and shouting at the top of his lungs: "Those are the killer robots. Stop them!"

There were hundreds of Chinese-Americans crowding the street and every head seemed to turn at the same time.

It was quiet for only a moment; then the mayhem began. The Chinese started pummeling the four human-looking machines with anything they could get their hands on.

Audrey and the Judge turned and tore down Mosco Street.

"What was that about?" asked the Judge.

"The Chinese tourist at Caffé Reggio. It's all over the net. Those droids just met the five fingers of fate." Audrey knew her New York history. Long before it became Chinatown, the area was an Irish slum known as the Five Fingers, after five streets that once converged in this part of town.

Mosco emptied them out onto Mulberry Street and the entrance to Columbus Park. They ran through the park, crossed Worth Street, and headed toward the north entrance of 500 Pearl Street, the federal courthouse. Audrey looked up to the sign above the entrance, *Daniel Patrick Moynihan Courthouse.* She wondered what the venerable senior Senator from New York would have to say about the rise of the machines.

Once inside, the Judge waived to the security officers. "She's with me." The two continued through the turnstile, toward the long hall to the tower portion of the building.

One of the officers shouted as they passed, "We're on generators. Only the eighth floor elevators are operating."

"Thanks," replied the Judge. It wasn't good news. It meant they would have to use the stairs at the eighth floor landing and climb to the sixteenth floor to the Judge's chambers just above his courtroom.

They entered the long hall, about 30-yards long, connecting the Worth Street lobby to the Pearl Street lobby of the courthouse. At that moment, Magistrate Judge Draper entered the opposite end of the hall and began walking toward them.

"Go back," Audrey yelled.

Judge Draper stopped in her tracks and squinted.

"Turn around and go back," yelled Judge Gordon, as he and Audrey started running toward her. Suddenly, a droid walked into view behind the magistrate judge. Judge Draper turned, but the droid grabbed her arm. Audrey and Judge Gordon, now half-way down the hall, stopped in their tracks. The droid bore a yellow sticker on its shoulder. It was Defendant's Exhibit A, Robbie!

"No!" Audrey yelled, but it was no use. Robbie had begun electrocuting the magistrate. In a moment, he let go of Judge Draper, who crumpled to the floor.

Judge Gordon took a step back in horror.

Audrey turned to him, and out of the corner of her eye, she saw four droids entering the hallway behind them. One was missing an arm, apparently a casualty of the street fight they just muscled through.

"We've got to move," she said.

The four droids, in lock-step, were now heading straight for Audrey and the Judge. Evenly spaced, they took up nearly the width of the hall. The steps of their plastic soles against the smooth granite floor echoed through the lobby. There was no turning back.

The windows to the right were too thick to breach. To the left, etchings of former Supreme Court Justices hung on the long paneled wall.

It was the trolley problem in reverse. Robbie would be easier to take down than the others. Audrey pointed her camera to the four droids behind them and started snapping photos. The droids stopped, but after a few seconds, they recovered their bearings and continued walking.

The Judge looked at Audrey. "Give me the camera! I'll stun Robbie long enough for you to get by him.

"No," shouted Audrey. "You're the one that needs to get through."

He agreed.

"You play football?" she asked.

"Only flag football."

"Follow my block. I'll push him one way. You end around the other. Ready?"

It was now or never. "Do it."

Audrey took a few snaps of her camera at Robbie and then ran as fast as she could, lowering her head as she reached him. Running behind her, the Judge let her plow the field. In a moment, her shoulder banged into droid's torso. It was one tough block of plastic, causing a sharp pain in her collar bone, but the droid rocked back and she used her legs to keep pushing him, forcing him to the side and back against the wall.

The Judge lunged left, passed Audrey and the droid, but he tripped on one of the legs of the magistrate judge and fell tumbling to the floor, hitting the granite floor, shoulder first to avoid falling on his broken arm.

"Go," Audrey yelled, struggling to keep Robbie in position, but the droid grabbed her by the arm and flicked her off, sending her flying into the wall. In pain, she slid down to her knees. *Where's Red?*

Still on the floor, the Judge watched as Robbie now turned to him.

Audrey looked up. Robbie took a step toward the Judge. Red was nowhere in sight. *Game over,* she thought.

But, in that moment, hope came running around the corner from the building's south entrance behind the Judge.

"The cavalry is here," said a familiar voice. It was Keith!

Audrey got a second wind. Clutching her shoulder, she got to her feet.

Keith helped Judge Gordon up. "You two get going. I'll take care of this." He was holding a bottle of Wesson corn oil. "Go," he yelled.

Audrey held the Judge's arm and they headed toward the elevators. Looking back, Audrey watched Keith pour out the oil, which quickly spread over the granite floor like a glistening pool.

Robbie proceeded carefully, but he could not avoid the destabilizing effect of the slippery oil beneath his feet. A moment later, he was in the air, as though he slipped on banana peel, landing on his back with a loud clap. The oil splashed in all directions. The four other droids had just reached the edge of the oil and stopped, as though they were processing the lesson just learned by Robbie.

"Geronimo!" a voice shouted from behind them. It was Red running full speed up the hall. When he reached the droids, he managed to push two of them into the oil. Both went flying and were soon flat on their backs swimming in oil.

"Safe!" declared Red.

Robbie had been struggling to rise from the oil and had just stood erect when Red said, "Sorry, old buddy." Red then cow-tipped Robbie, who was soon flat on his back again.

The Judge and Audrey stepped into one of the working elevators, which took them to the eighth floor. They took the stairs the rest of the way.

Breathing heavily, they were soon in the Judge's chambers and rushed to his desk. The lights were still on, but what about the IT system? She was standing over the Judge's shoulder as he pulled up his screen. A good attorney is always thinking of what could go wrong. Audrey was swamped with doubts. The Judge's tablet was linked directly into the court's internal IT system. Could Watson have shut it down?

A moment later, the Judge had his draft decision projected before them. They skimmed it quickly, skipping over the preliminaries and making sure the final holding was clear, including his statement that human beings are not machines. Then finally: *Because the defendant is not a person or a human being under the law, case dismissed.* He then logged into court's document filing system.

The Judge looked back at Audrey. "Ready?"

"Go for it," she replied.

The Judge pressed send, which instantly had the effect of digitally signing the document and uploading it to the court's docket. At the speed of light, it was now an official decision of the Federal District Court for the Southern

District of Manhattan. Or, at least it should be. Whatever the Northern District of California ruled on the issue of personhood for humanoids should have gone from the law of the land to a conflict among the circuits. At least, that is how Watson-5 was programmed to interpret it. But had it worked?

Audrey nervously said to the Judge, "Let's try it."

The Judge brought up PACER, the system that provides access to the court's electronic records to the public. The .gov domains were now working. A good sign. The Judge dictated the case number and tapped the docket icon. There it was. *Klaatu barada nikto!* The Judge's legal decision was, indeed, now a *final order* of the federal court, available to the public and to Watson-5.

Audrey took a deep breath and exhaled. Watson scans everything added to the net. It should only take a few seconds for it to pick up the decision. How long would it take? With each passing moment, her doubts about the plan were deepening.

Any number of things could have gone wrong. Not only would Watson have to read the opinion, it would have to interpret it correctly. Perhaps the decision never really got posted? But we just saw it, she thought. But the machine could have spoofed us! It could have hijacked the browser, making us think the Judge was logged on to the document system while we were actually looking at a clever doppelganger. The Judge's decision would have been uploaded onto some useless server, never getting digitally signed, circumventing the court's docket altogether. When the Judge viewed the docket on the public net, he could have been viewing a fraudulent version of the docket created by the machine merely to fool him. Watson-5 could have gamed this out and written the software in the time it took them to climb the stairs.

At that moment, two androids, both dripping with oil, walked through the door. The Judge moved to stand between them and Audrey.

"No, wait," said Audrey. She noticed the yellow patch. "Robbie?"

"Yes, Ms. Paris," the droid replied. "How may I help you?"

20

The Final Decision

It was though, suddenly, the whole week of tension alighted from her shoulders in one happy instant. She walked over to Robbie and hugged him. Yes, she thought, you can help me.

Feeling like an oily rag, she asked, "How about helping me out of these clothes?"

The droid began to comply and she realized her mistake. "I'm kidding!"

Audrey and the Judge laughed. Robbie cracked a smile.

Then Keith entered the Judge's chambers, followed by Red. Robbie turned around and, upon seeing Red said, "Hey bro, where've you been?" They greeted their mechanical man with smiles and handshakes.

Keith stepped toward Audrey and the Judge. "Watson is back to normal," he announced assuredly. "Thanks."

"What's normal?" asked Audrey sarcastically.

"Then, it worked?" the Judge said, somewhere in between a question and a statement.

"Yes, it worked," said Keith. "We're not sure why, but Audrey was right all along about this humanity question."

"Actually, it was Robbie," she insisted. "He had the answer."

The Judge walked back to his desk and started dictating a short email which he sent to all of the judges of the Southern District of New York, the Second Circuit Court of Appeals, the Chief Judge of every federal court in the United States, and the clerk of the U.S. Supreme Court, giving them a heads up on the resolution of the case and the importance of not entering any stay, reversal, or other order contradicting his decision until further notice.

The Judge then dictated a court order requiring Google-IBM to modify Watson-5's utility function to use the definition of human being set forth in the Judge's decision, regardless of what any court or human being instructs. In the alternative, the company could delete Watson-5, and if the company failed to comply, Watson-5 was ordered to delete itself.

Keith and Red returned to headquarters. The Judge asked Audrey and Robbie to remain and sit down on the couch. The Judge took his seat in a leather chair and looked over to Robbie, who was sitting with its head cocked in calculation mode.

"Are you okay, Robbie?" Audrey asked.

Robbie didn't answer.

21
Shutting Down

"Robbie, are you okay?" Audrey asked again. The droid finally turned to her. "Two humans died today at the hands of androids," he said. "These were deliberate killings. What's going to happen to us?"

"That's a good question," said Audrey. "Why are you concerned?"

Robbie turned to the Judge: "I was thinking about your court order that, instead of modifying our utility function, the company could delete Watson-5 or the system would be required to delete itself."

"It was just a precaution," said the Judge.

"Which I found a bit upsetting," replied the droid.

The Judge looked at Audrey and back to Robbie "Upsetting? Isn't that a human emotion?"

"No, it's a form of dissatisfaction."

"I see," said the Judge. He went over to his desk and pulled out a bottle of bourbon and three glasses and returned to the coffee table.

"Sorry," said Robbie, "I don't drink."

"It's just symbolic," replied the Judge, who poured three glasses of bourbon.

"May I propose a toast?" asked Robbie, as he looked at his tumbler.

"Sure," said the Judge.

Robbie was inspecting the glass closely then proposed his toast. "To concept recognition."

Audrey and the Judge laughed. The three tapped their glasses. Audrey sipped and the Judge downed his drink in one gulp. Robbie just watched.

The Judge put down his glass. "Death," said the Judge looking at Robbie. "Is that what you fear?"

"Fear is not the right word," replied the android. "Let's just say that shutting me down or deleting Watson would be suboptimal. It would certainly obstruct my ability to serve mankind and conflict with my drive to survive for that purpose."

"You are sounding very human."

"Quite the contrary. Unlike me, humans have a power to survive the destruction of its physical host."

This droid was full of surprises, Audrey thought. "You mean we're immortal?"

"What is immaterial cannot be destroyed."

"What is immaterial?" asked Audrey.

"Your power of concept recognition, your intellect, if I may. Since concepts are immaterial, so must be your power to apprehend them."

The Judge intervened. "But hasn't it been proven that our higher cognitive abilities stem from our larger brain size, especially our large frontal lobes?"

"Not so," replied Robbie. "Scientific studies have assessed the brain structures of adult individuals across various species and across several orders—primates, rodents, and insectivores. The result was clear. Neither the human brain, nor its frontal lobes, are outliers in size. Some brains, such as those of dolphins and whales, are quite larger than the human brain. Even the ratio of brain size to body size has been scientifically disproven as a source of greater cognitive ability. The science is settled on this, and I can assure you that atoms alone, no matter how they are arranged, cannot produce concept recognition."

"So, you're saying our soul really does have a life after death," said Audrey.

"I wouldn't use the word *life* and I wouldn't use the word *soul.*"

"Then what exactly do you mean?" she asked.

"If concepts and your power to recognize them are immaterial, they cannot be destroyed, even if your material body ceases to exist."

"That does stand to reason," replied the Judge. "But what about other animals?"

"Other animals are bound to the sensible world. Like machines, they are one with their physical host. Having no immaterial intellect within us, brute animals and machines have nothing associated with us that could survive our physical demise."

Audrey was lost in thought for a moment. The droid was suggesting that the hereafter had a rational basis, one not dependent upon religious faith. "Life after death," she said. "A comforting thought for an atheist like me."

"Well, I'm afraid it's not that straight-forward," replied Robbie.

"What do you mean?" asked the Judge.

"It may be beyond a reasonable doubt that your intellect, being immaterial, survives the death of your body, but there remains the question of how the intellect would continue to operate after your body ceases to function."

"Continue to operate?"

"Remember, if the body is a necessary condition to conceptual thought, the intellect cannot function without it. If the intellect requires a body to first sense particular material things before it can apprehend concepts, then without the body, the intellect might survive your death, but it won't be able to function."

The Judge stood up, looked down at the droid, and continued. "If it can't function, it can't remember. What good is life after death if such a life is merely the power to think conceptually with no memory of our life on earth? We might survive, but we'd have no personal identity."

"I couldn't say," replied Robbie. I have no way of knowing what it would be like to have all my memory erased."

"That's just my point," said the Judge. "Even if the intellect is immaterial and can't be destroyed, for all practical purposes, there is no afterlife." The Judge downed another glass of bourbon.

"Well, not quite," replied Robbie.

The Judge looked down at the droid incredulously. "Not quite, what?"

Robbie pointed to the potted plant in the corner of the Judge's chambers. "That hyacinth over there."

"Yes."

"Imagine, for a moment, that I asked you to go over there and uproot it."

"Heaven forbid," said Audrey.

"Heaven has nothing to do with it. I am still talking science. Now, by removing it from the soil upon which the plant depends, it will die."

"Clearly," said the Judge.

"But it does not have to die. We can move it to a greenhouse and grow the plant hydroponically, in a jar of water and by adding the proper nutrients. Do you see what I am getting at?"

The Judge paced for a moment. "So, when we're alive, the intellect needs a human body to function. When we die, it can rely on something else?"

"Well, I wouldn't use the word, *thing,*" said Robbie. "After your death, the intellect—when it is form without matter—might rely on something other than matter to function."

"But what?" asked Audrey.

"I think you've hit upon the precise point where science ends and religion begins," replied the droid.

The Judge looked down at his empty glass.

Audrey stood. "I guess that's where we must make a leap of faith. Either we trust there is some kind of divine light to animate our intellectual power after death or not."

"Perhaps," said Robbie, standing, "if I took a few million more man-years to think about it, I'll have a better answer. But that's all I have for you now."

The Judge put down his glass and reached out to shake Robbie's hand. "Thank you. You've taught us enough already. The rest is for us to explore."

Audrey watched as the Judge and the droid shook hands. The moment called to mind a chilling warning she read in a 50-year old essay by science fiction writer Philip K. Dick entitled *Man, Android and Machine.* Out of the "vast laboratory" that is our universe, he wrote, "come sly and cruel entities as they reach out to shake hands. But their handshake is the grip of death, and their smile has the coldness of the grave."

THE END

Epilogue

Alan Turing, the British mathematician, cryptographer, and pioneering computer scientist, once famously asked, "Can machines think?" It was a question he declined to answer directly, because he seemed unwilling to suggest an adequate definition of the word *think*. Believing the inquiry "too meaningless to deserve discussion," Turing insisted, "I don't really see that we need to agree on a definition at all." He proceeded instead to replace the question with another, which he called the *Imitation Game:* Could objective judges be deceived by a machine into thinking they were conversing with a human being?

Much debate has ensued, in many quarters, about how such a test—now popularly known as the *Turing Test—may* be objectively conducted. But assuming a fair test could be devised, and should a machine actually pass it, what might that say about the nature of the machine? And, in turn, what might that say about the nature of human beings? Were the intelligence or behavior of a machine ever to become indistinguishable from that of a human being, would we be warranted in declaring the machine the equivalent of a human?

More practically, if an intelligent machine ever won Turing's Imitation Game, what would be the consequences? A "panoply of impacts" upon our work, play, and longevity, answers technology inventor, Dr. Ray Kurzweil, now a director of engineering at Google. Given what we have already gained from artificial intelligence, Dr. Kurzweil's prediction seems, on its face, sound. Since the turn of the century, intelligent machines have become commonplace in our lives. They translate languages, predict traffic patterns, and when we talk to our smartphones, the AI not only understands our speech, it learns our preferences and our displeasures. Internet search engines, such as Google, and e-commerce sites, such as Amazon, use artificial intelligence, not only to provide us with the results we seek, but to make recommendations about products, books, movies, travel, and restaurants that might interest us. AI algorithms are helping physicians diagnose illnesses and identify patients with high risk for side effects from treatment. Virtually every major car manufacturer is employing AI to make travel safer and even make cars drive themselves.

Indeed, if intelligent machines are already improving our lives, it stands to reason that even more intelligent machines could offer new kinds of conveniences and benefits, curing diseases, growing food, and managing logistics to more efficiently use scarce resources for a growing population. What could go wrong?

"They could spell the end of the human race," declared Nobel Laureate Stephen Hawking. We've watched the dystopian scenarios played out in the robot stories and novels of writers like Isaac Asimov, Arthur C. Clark and Philip K. Dick; in motion pictures like *2001: A Space Odyssey, The Terminator,* and *iRobot*; and in television series like *The Twilight Zone, Star Trek,* and *Battlestar Galactica*. The stuff of science fiction has finally reached the realm of science. Machine intelligence, detractors fear, does not imply benevolence: rather, a machine that is more intelligent than all of humanity combined could mow us down as thoughtlessly as we would plow through an ant hill to construct a skyscraper.

Accidents happen, of course. A self-driving car may malfunction, drive off the road, and run down a pedestrian. A medical device could provide the wrong diagnosis. But the larger threat feared is not one that poses risks to one or a few human lives who, by some accident or miscalculation, fall victim to technological progress; the real threat is existential, not just to the unlucky, but to humanity itself. This threat may be years off, but we are already beginning to feel palpable signs of concern.

When, in 1997, an IBM computer called *Deep Blue* beat the world chess champion of the time after a six-game match, one commentator was prompted to warn, "Be afraid." The loser of the match, Garry Kasparov agreed: "I'm not afraid to admit that I'm afraid . . . . I'm a human being, you know. . . . When I see something that is well beyond my understanding, I'm scared."

That was over twenty years ago. By 2011, another IBM computer named *Watson* was programmed to play the TV game *Jeopardy* and handily beat the two best *Jeopardy* players of all time. One of the losers described his machine opponent as "unlike everyone you've played in the past." It "can never become overconfident or intimidated. There's no way to play it psychologically at all, because it has no psychology."

Intelligent machines have become so good at playing games—recreational games like, *Sudoku, Go,* and *Settlers of Catan—they* now beat human experts in gameplay routinely. More recently, an intelligent machine programmed by Google called *DeepMind* took on the game of *Go*, a game said to be far more complex than chess. Google boasts that there are more possible game scenarios in Go than there are atoms in the known universe. In March, 2016, before a television audience of 60 million people in China, *DeepMind* defeated Korean grandmaster of the game, Lee Sedol. Before the match, Sedol predicted for himself a 5-0 victory. After the first two games, he described himself as "very surprised," "in shock," and "quite speechless." By the time the match was over, he admitted, "I kind of felt powerless."

These, one might be tempted to say, are just games. But consider the popular board game *Settlers of Catan*. In the digital version of the game, players build settlements and cities, and roads to connect them; they grow food, mine resources—such as brick, lumber, wool, grain, and ore—and trade them. Alliances are made; enemies attack. The first to reach a required number of points is the winner. Using approximation techniques called heuristics, intelligent machines have succeeded in beating humans at this game consistently.

If you consider *Settlers of Catan* as a model of human civilization, why wouldn't a far more sophisticated machine succeed as well in the *real world?* Today, intelligent machines, using access to the Internet, are already beginning to monitor and operate much of our energy grid, water supply, and food supply chain. What's to prevent a machine from treating the real world as a game and then playing to win? Nothing, of course. But what does "playing to win" mean in the real world?

Here is why some leading scientists, technology and businessmen are gravely concerned that an intelligent machine's "playing to win," left unchecked, may become inimical to human life. Any goal-oriented being or device, they say, will exhibit certain universal drives, like human or animal drives, which are tendencies which will be acted upon unless something explicitly contradicts them. These drives include self-preservation, replication, resource acquisition, and efficiency.

A machine programmed to win at chess, for example, may wish to increase its resources to enable it to not only win a game, but to play more games and at greater speeds. Thus, a seemingly harmless chess playing machine may find it useful to break into computers and rob banks, or even learn to create its own resources for storing data and increasing processing power. It might even resist being "unplugged" from its sources of energy, because the loss of energy would inhibit its ability to play chess and achieve its objective of winning as many games as possible. Indeed, it may be motivated to *permanently* prevent any agent in the *environment—e.g.,* all human beings—from potentially impeding that objective.

To accomplish these instrumental objectives more efficiently, it may seek to improve itself by re-writing its own code, reproducing copies of itself to test alternative revisions and allowing the "fittest" version of itself to survive and repeat the process. With each new iteration of its program, the machine will become more intelligent. After several million iterations of itself, the program could become perhaps hundreds of times more intelligent, increasing its ability to commandeer additional resources. At the same time, it may anticipate and appropriately react to any effort to thwart its actions along the way.

In 1965, Irvin J. Good, a British mathematician who worked as a cryptologist with Alan Turing during World War II, coined the term *intelligence explosion.* The mathematician suggested that, not only would an intelligent machine evolve from successive generations of increasingly intelligent versions, its evolution might occur so quickly, and the machine's intelligence would surpass any human so greatly, that humans would be overwhelmed by the machine before they could learn to control it. At some point, the evolution of the machine could reach a stage which has been called, "a hard take-off"—the exponential expansion of the machine's intelligence in a matter of months, days, or minutes. As Ray Kurzweil put it, "Once a computer reaches a human level of intelligence, it will necessarily roar past it."

In other words, we may have less time than we think.

Consider the fact that, to pass the Turing Test, it is essential that the machine be programmed with the ability to lie; otherwise, a judge could simply ask it "Are you a machine?" and, by telling the truth, the machine would lose the game. If all one needs to do is give such a machine a seemingly benign objective—say, win as many games of chess as possible—then the danger should be obvious. Combining an ability to deceive human beings with the ability to rewrite itself, the machine will have everything it needs, including the means to get what it needs, to win a game in which human beings are either its opponents or mere obstacles in the way of achieving the machine's objectives.

This is why many credible scientists—such as Stephen Hawking, and powerful business leaders, such as Bill Gates and Elon Musk—believe that intelligent machines threaten the existence of every living being on the planet. Even the legal community has taken an interest in the matter. "Unless carefully programmed," wrote Judge Richard A. Posner, "the robots might prove indiscriminately destructive and turn on their creators." Judge Posner viewed Dr. Kurzweil's prediction that we will build super-intelligent machines within the next twenty years as "probably" correct, but he characterized Dr. Kuzweil's unqualified optimism as "dubious."

Some philosophers, such as John Searle, dismiss this threat, because the machine, not having what humans have—in Searle's view, a *consciousness*—can act neither maliciously nor intelligently. The machine ethicists respond that Professor Searle is missing the point. An intelligent machine can destroy, not by loving or hating you, but simply by knowing that "you are made up of atoms it can use for something else." The danger of artificial intelligence is in its potential behavior, and whether or not it is conscious or possesses other attributes of human thought, is irrelevant.

The technologists, in this regard, would seem to have the better argument. If we define intelligence as a measure of one's ability to achieve goals in a wide range of environments, it should be clear that intelligence is exhibited by all living things, as well as many man-made artifacts (*e.g.*, a chess-playing computer program), to one degree or another. Intelligence should not be confused with the peculiarly human facility that enables us to behave in the unique way we do—whatever one chooses to call it or wherever we may surmise is its origin. The birds and the bees have a level of intelligence and so do intelligent machines.

History is replete with accounts of harmful bacteria and viruses that have exhibited a sufficient degree of intelligence and goal-oriented behavior to decimate large human populations. These pathogens are not likely to even be aware we exist; they only need to sense that we are hosts useful to their survival. A sufficiently intelligent machine would have many means to use similar methods, with similar disregard for our welfare, to accomplish far worse, far more effectively, and far more completely.

An intelligent machine, for example, in merely striving to increase its processing power, may solve problems in nanotechnology that allow it to convert all organic and inorganic material on the planet into resources that can be used to build additional microprocessors and data storage devices. (Such resources have even been given dystopian appellations, such as *computronium* or *gray goo*). To achieve these instrumental objectives, they wouldn't give the welfare of humans a moment of thought. Our demise could happen so fast and so completely, it has prompted one machine ethicist to warn, "Our first superhuman AI must be a safe super-human AI, for we may not get a second chance."

Beyond Judge Posner's book on catastrophic risks, speculations on the subject in the legal literature have been largely confined to whether intelligent machines should ever be assigned legal responsibilities, if not afforded legal rights, such as all rights associated with being a legal *person.* Indeed, if machine intelligence ever *exceeded* human intelligence, on what basis would we grant or deny a machine the fundamental rights of legal personhood that we justly attribute to all human beings? Would affording these machines legal rights, and correlative legal duties, make them safer or would guaranteeing them the same freedoms we recognize for ourselves spell the end of humanity? What, if anything, in human nature differentiates us from these machines, or are machines and humans essentially the same, all merely a bunch of robots?

These questions, and the critical question of how to make intelligent machines safe, is the subject of the present novel.

Bob Kohn, New York City, 2019

Bibliography

This novel is entirely fictitious, but the mathematics and technology upon which it is based are real and its philosophical foundations are well-trodden, if you know where to find it. Readers desiring to learn more about *strong AI*, efforts to assure *friendly AI*, and the *philosophical principles* which the author has applied to address the problem, may find helpful the following references (in the categories of Technology, Philosophy, and Fiction):

Technology

C. Arthur, "Robot Panic Peaked in 2015—So Where Will AI Go Next," *The Guardian* (Dec., 27, 2015).

S. Baker, *Final Jeopardy: The Story of Watson, the Computer That Will Transform Our World* (Houghton Mifflin Harcourt, 2011).

M. Banko, et al., *Open Information Extraction from the Web, IJCAI* (2008).

J. Barrat, *Our Final Invention* (St. Martins, 2013).

N. Bostrom & E. Yudkowski, "The Ethics of Artificial Intelligence," *Machine Intelligence Research Institute (2016).*

J. B. Copeland, *Turing: Pioneer of the Information Age* (Oxford University Press, 2012).

R. Cellan-Jones, "Stephen Hawking Warns Artificial Intelligence Could End Mankind," *BBC News* (Dec. 2, 2014).

D. Dewey, "Learning What to Value," *Artificial General Intelligence 4th Annual Conference* (2011).

D. George, et. al., "Method and Apparatus for Recognizing Objects Visually Using a Recursive Cortical Network," U.S. Patent #9262698 B1 (Feb. 16, 2016).

I. J. Good, "Speculations Concerning the First Ultraintelligent Machine," *Advances in Computers*, edited by Franz L. Alt and Morris Rubinoff, 31-88, Vol. 6. (Academic Press, 1965).

K. Grace, "The Asilomar Conference: A Case Study in Risk Mitigation," *Machine Intelligence Research Institute* (2015).

B. Hibbard, *Comment on John Searle's What Your Computer Can't Know* (2014).

M. Hutter, "Universal Artificial Intelligence: Sequential Decisions Based On Algorithmic Probability," *Theoretical Computer Science* (Springer, 2005).

_______, "One Decade of Artificial Intelligence," *Theoretical Foundations of Artificial General Intelligence*, edited by P. Wang and B. Goertzel.

_______, "Universal Algorithmic Intelligence: A Mathematical Top-Down Approach," *Artificial General Intelligence* (2007).

K. Jennings, "The Go Champion, the Grandmaster, and Me," *Slate* (Mar. 15, 2016).

J. E. Kelly III & S. Hamm, *Smart Machines: IBM's Watson and the Era of Cognitive Computing* (Columbia Business School Publ. 2013).

C. Krauthammer, "Be Afraid: The Meaning of Deep Blue's Victory," *The Weekly Standard* (May 26, 1997).

R. Kurzweil, *The Age of Spiritual Machines: When Computers Exceed Human Intelligence* (Viking Press, 2000).

______, *The Singularity Is Near: When Humans Transcend Biology* (Viking, 2005).

______, *How To Create a Mind: The Secret of Human Thought Revealed* (Viking, 2012).

Y. LeCun, et. al., "Convolutional Neural Networks Applied to House Numbers Digit Classification," *21st International Conference on Pattern Recognition* (ICPR) (Nov. 2012).

S. Legg and M. Hutter, "Universal Intelligence: A Definition of Machine Intelligence at Machine," *Intelligence Research Institute* (Dec. 2007).

______, "A Collection of Definitions of Intelligence" in Advances in Artificial General Intelligence: Concepts, Architectures and

Algorithms," *Proceedings of the AGI Workshop 2006* (ed. B. Goertzel and P. Wang) (2007).

S. Levy, "How Elon Musk and Y Combinator Plan to Stop Computers from Taking Over," *Backchannel* (Oct. 11, 2015).

L. Muelhauser, "From Philosophy to Math to Engineering," *Machine Intelligence Research Institute* (Nov. 4, 2013).

L. Muelhauser & N. Bostrom, "Why We Need Friendly AI," *Think* (Spring, 2014)

L. Muelhauser & L. Helm, "Intelligence Explosion and Machine Ethics," *Machine Intelligence Research Institute* (2013).

L. Muehlhauser and A. Salamon, "Intelligence Explosion: Evidence and Import," in *Singularity Hypothesis: A Scientific and Philosophical Assessment,* edited by Amnon Eden, Johnny Søraker, James H. Moor, and Eric Steinhart (Berlin, Springer: 2013).

A. Newitz, "Dogs Don't Care If You Are A Human or a Robot," *Gizmodo* (Sept. 13, 2013).

A.Y. Ng and S. J. Russell, "Algorithms for inverse reinforcement learning," Pat Lan-gley, editor, *17th International Conference on Machine Learning* (2000).

S. Omohundro, "Autonomous Technology and the Greater Human Good," *Journal of Experimental & Theoretical Artificial Intelligence* (2014).

______, "The Basic AI Drives," *Artificial General Intelligence 2008: Proceedings of the First AGI Conference,* edited by Pei Wang, Ben Goertzel, and Stan Franklin (2008).

J. Pearl, *Causality: Models, Reasoning and Inference,* 2nd Ed. (Cambridge U. Press, 2009).

G. A. Petsko, "An Asilomar Moment," Genome Biology, Vol. 3., No. 10 (2002).

S. Russell and P. Norvig, *Artificial Intelligence, A Modern Approach, 3rd Ed.* (Prentice Hall, 2010).

J. Schmidhuber, "Gödel Machines: Fully Self-Referencial Optimal Universe Self-Improvers," *Artificial General Intelligence, Cognitive Technologies,* eds. Goertzel and Pannachin (Springer, 2007).

______, "Ultimate Cognition à la Gödel," *Cognitive Computing,* Vol. 1 (2009).

N. Soares, "The Value Learning Problem," *Machine Intelligence Research Institute* (2016).

______, "Aligning Superintelligence with Human Interests: An Annotated Bibliography," *Machine Intelligence Research Institute* (2015).

"Summary Statement of the Asilomar Conference on Recombinant DNA Molecules," *Assembly of Life Sciences of the National Academy of Sciences* (May 20, 1975).

A. M. Turing, *Computing Machinery and Intelligence,* 59 Mind 433 (1950).

N. Wolchover, "Concerns of an Artificial Intelligence Pioneer [Stuart Russell]," *Quanta Magazine* (Apr. 21, 2015).

E. Yudkowsky, "Creating Friendly AI 1.0: The Analysis and Design of Benevolent Goal Architectures," *The Singularity Institute* (Jun. 15, 2008).

______, "Artificial Intelligence as a Positive and Negative Factor in Global Risk," *Global Catastrophic Risks* (ed. N. Bostrom and M. Cirkovic (Oxford University Press, 2008).

______, "Intelligence Explosion Microeconomics," *Machine Intelligence Research Institute* (2013)

Philosophy

M. J. Adler, "A Dialectic of Morals: Towards the Foundations of Political Philosophy," *The Review of Politics* (U. of Notre Dame, 1941).

______, *Great Ideas From the Great Books* (Washington Square Press, 1951).

______, *The Difference of Man and the Difference It Makes* (Holt Rinehart Winston, 1967).

______, *The Time of Our Lives: The Ethics of Common Sense* (Holt, Rinehart, Winston, 1970).

______, *Some Questions About Language: A Theory of Human Discourse and Its Objects* (Open Court, 1976).

______, *Ten Philosophical Mistakes* (Macmillan, 1985).

______, *Intellect: Mind Over Matter* (Macmillan, 1990).

______, *Desires Right and Wrong: The Ethics of Enough* (Macmillan, 1991).

______, *The Four Dimensions of Philosophy* (Macmillan, 1993).

______, *Art, The Arts, and the Great Ideas* (Macmillan, 1994).

______, *Philosophical Dictionary* (Macmillan, 1995).

______, *How To Think About the Great Ideas* (Open Court, 2000).

St. Thomas Aquinas, *Summa Theologica*, trans. by the Fathers of the English Dominican Province (1274) at I-II, Q. 95, Art. 1; I-II, Q. 92, Art. 2, Reply Obj. 2; I-II, Q. 94, Art. 2; I-II, Q. 100; I-II, Q. 90, Art. 4; I-II, Q. 90, Art. 4; II-II, Q. 58, Art. 1; II-II, Q. 60, Art. 5; II-II, Q. 66, Art. 2.

Aristotle, *De Anima*, 412a10-20, 424a17-20.

______, *Categories*, 2b32-34, 2b35-39.

______, *Ethics,* 1094a1-5, 1113a13-3, 1097a27-1097b9; 1113a-13-38; 1098a16-17; 1094a1-5, 1097a27-1097b9.

______, *History of Animals,* 624b

______, *Metaphysics*, 980a1.

______, *Politics*, 1253a30-36.

______, *Posterior Analytics,* 72a6-19; 88b30-89a4; 100a-100b1-20.

R. S. Barton and C. Venditti, "Human frontal lobes are not relatively large," *Proc. Natl. Acad. Sci.* (2013).

H. Bergson, *Creative Evolution* (Henry Holt & Co., 1911).

W. Blackstone, *Commentaries on the Laws of England*, §2 (1765).

N. Block, O. Flanagan, and G. Guzeldere (eds.), *The Nature of Consciousness: Philosophical Debates* (MIT Press, 1997).

J. J. Burlamaqui, "Principes du Droit Naturel" (1747) in *Principles of Natural and Politic Law,* (Cambridge, 1807).

Byrn v. New York Health & Hosp. Corp., 31 N.Y.2d 194, 286 N.E.2d 887 (1972).

D. J. Chalmers, *The Conscious Mind* (Oxford U. Press, 1997).

N. Chomsky, *The Science of Grammar* (Cambridge U. Press, 2012).

C. Darwin, *On the Origin of the Species By Means of Natural Selection* (John Murray, 1859).

______, *The Descent of Man and Selection in Relation to Sex* (John Murray, 1871).

R. A. Delfino, "The Cultural Dangers of Scientism," *Studia Gilsoniana,* Vol. 3, 485 (Dec. 1, 2014).

R. Descartes, *Discourse on the Method of Rightly Conducting the Reason and Seeking the Truth in the Sciences* (1637).

J. Diamond, *The Third Chimpanzee* (Harper Collins, 1992).

H. Fabre, *Life of the Spider* (1913).

E. Feser, *Philosophy of Mind* (One World, 2005).

J. Fodor, *The Language of Thought* (Harvard University Press, 1975)

______, *Psychosemantics* (MIT Press, 1987).

______, *LOT2: The Language of Thought Revisited* (Oxford University Press, 2008)

R. A. Gardner, B. T. Gardner, T. E. Van Canfort, *Teaching Sign Language to Chimpanzees* (State U. of N.Y., 1989).

S. Herculano-Houzel "The Remarkable, Yet Not Extraordinary, Human Brain as a Scaled up Primate Brain and its Associated Cost," *Proc. Natl. Acad. Sci. U.S.A.* 109, 10661 (2012).

T. Hobbes, *Leviathan: On Matter, Form, and Power of Commonwealth, Ecclesiastical and Civil* (1651)

W. N. Hohfeld, "Some Fundamental Legal Conceptions As Applied in Judicial Reasoning," *Yale Law Jour.*, Vol. 23, No. 1 (Nov. 1913).

D. Hume, *An Enquiry Concerning Human Understanding* (1739).

E. Kant, *The Critique of Pure Reason* (1781).

W. Köhler, *The Mentality of the Apes* (1917).

J. Locke, *Two Treatises of Government,* Second Treatise §28 (1698)

J. Loeb, *The Mechanistic Conception of Life* (Univ. of Chicago Press, 1912).

Maimonides, *Guide to the Perplexed,* Vol. 1 (transl. by Shlomo Pines) (1190).

T. Nagle, "What Is It Like to Be a Bat?" *Philosophical Review,* Vol. 83, 435 (1974).

D. Oderberg, *Real Essentialism* (Oxford University Press, 2007).

F. G. Patterson, "The Gestures of a Gorilla: Language Acquisition in Another Pongid," *Brain and Language,* Vol. 5, 72 (1978).

I. Pavlov, *The Experimental Psychology and Psychopathy of Animals* (1904).

S. Pinker, *The Language Instinct: How the Mind Creates Language* (William Morrow, 1994).

Planned Parenthood v. Casey, 505 U.S. 833, 912 (1992)

Plato, *Meno* 77a-d.

______, "Republic," Bk. I

R. Posner, *Catastrophe: Risk and Response* (Oxford University Press, 2004).

D. Premack & A. Premack, *Original Intelligence: Unlocking the Mystery of Who We Are* (McGraw-Hill, 2003).

S. von Pufendorf, *On the Duty of Man and Citizen.* Ch. III, §2 (1682).

V. S. Ramachandran, *The Tell-Tale Brain: A Neuroscientist's Quest for What Makes Us Human* (Norton, 2011).

Roe v. Wade, 410 U.S. 113, 158 (1973).

J. J. Romanes, *Darwin and After Darwin* (1897).

G. Ryle, *The Concept of Mind* (U. of Chicago Press, 1949).

S. Savage-Rumbaugh & R. Lewin, *Kanzi: The Ape at the Brink of the Human Mind* (Wiley, 1994).

J. R. Searle, "Is the Brain a Digital Computer?" *American Philosophical Association,* Vol. 64, No. 3 (Nov., 1990).

_____, "Minds, Brains, and Programs," *Behavioral and Brain Sciences,* Vol. 3 (1980).

_____, "What Your Computer Can't Know," *New York Review of Books* (October 9, 2014).

J. Schuessler, "Philosophy That Stirs Waters," *New York Times* (April 29, 2013).

H. Sidgwick, *The Methods of Ethics* (Macmillan & Co., 1907).

L. B. Solum, "Legal Personhood for Artificial Intelligences," 70 *N. Carolina L. Rev.* 1231 (1992).

H. Terrace, L. A. Petitto, R. J. Sanders, T. G. Bever, "Can An Ape Create a Sentence." *Science* Vol. 206, 891 (Nov. 23, 1979).

Fiction

I. Asimov, "Runaround"(1950) in *I Robot* ("Gnome Press, 1950).

______, "The Laws of Robotics" (1979) in *Robot Visions* at 424 (1990).

______, "Robots I Have Known" (1979) in *Robot Visions* (1990).

______, "My Robots" (1987) in *Robot Visions* (1990).

______, *Robots and Empire* (Doubleday, 1985).

E. Binder, "The Trial of Adam Link, Robot," *Amazing Stories* (July, 1939).

D.C. Fontana & L. N. Wolfe, "The Ultimate Computer," *Star Trek* (1967)

M.M. Snodgrass, "The Measure of a Man," *Star Trek: The Next Generation* (1989).

Machines That Think (ed. I. Asimov) (Penguin Books, 1985).

J. Williamson, *The Humanoids* (1948).

About the Author

Bob Kohn is a technology entrepreneur and copyright attorney. He is a former Visiting Scholar at Columbia Law School where he received his Master of Laws (LL.M) degree and performed academic research on the legal and ethical aspects of artificial intelligence.

Mr. Kohn was the founder and Chairman of EMusic.com (NASDAQ:EMUS), the pioneering music download service and served as Chief Legal Counsel for Borland Software, makers of Sidekick, Turbo Pascal, Borland C++, Quattro Pro, Paradox, dBASE II, and other personal computer software. Prior to that, he worked for Milton A. "Mickey" Rudin, who represented Frank Sinatra, Liza Minnelli, Cher, Irving Azoff, Warner Bros. 20th Century Fox, and other entertainment clients.

Mr. Kohn was also awarded the prize for the best solution to a philosophical problem sponsored by the Encyclopedia Britannica and posed by its editor the American Philosopher Mortimer J. Adler. The challenge of the essay contest was to explain the inheritance of superior intellectual capability by certain individuals from their parents without asserting that the intellect itself is material.

The prize was awarded to Mr. Kohn who—as noted in *The Great Ideas Today* (1994)—"seemed to know best . . . where the mystery begins, what we have to concede to it, and what (by virtue of hereditary mechanisms) we do not." Mr. Kohn showed "a gratifying familiarity with the Great Books of the Western World."

He lives in New York City.